D1548153

Radicalizing Enactivism

Radicalizing Enactivism

Basic Minds without Content

Daniel D. Hutto and Erik Myin

The MIT Press
Cambridge, Massachusetts
London, England

MIT Press books may be purchased at special quantity discounts for business or sales promotional use. For information, please email special_sales@mitpress.mit.edu or write to Special Sales Department, The MIT Press, 55 Hayward Street, Cambridge, MA 02142.

Set in Stone Sans and Stone Serif by The MIT Press. Printed and bound in the United States of America.

Library of Congress Cataloging-in-Publication Data
Hutto, Daniel D.
Radicalizing enactivism : basic minds without content / Daniel D. Hutto and Erik Myin.
     p.   cm.
Includes bibliographical references (p.) and index.
ISBN 978-0-262-01854-8 (hardcover : alk. paper)
1. Cognition—Philosophy. 2. Philosophy and cognitive science.
3. Philosophy of mind. 4. Cognitive science. 5. Content (Psychology)
I. Myin, Erik. II. Title.
BF311.H89   2013
128'.2—dc23
2012016253

10 9 8 7 6 5 4 3 2 1

for our wives, Farah and Inez, and our children, the three
Hutto boys and the three Myin girls

ad augusta per angusta

Contents

Preface

Man is so intelligent that he feels impelled to invent theories to account for what happens in the world. Unfortunately, he is not quite intelligent enough, in most cases, to find correct explanations.
—Aldous Huxley

The deepest sin against the human mind is to believe things without evidence.
—Thomas Henry Huxley

Catching a swirling leaf, finding one's way through unfamiliar terrain, attending and keeping track of another's gaze, watching the sun rising at the horizon—the vast sea of what humans do and experience is best understood by appealing to dynamically unfolding, situated embodied interactions and engagements with worldly offerings.

Where we find such familiar activity we find basic minds. But, we propose, the nature of the mentality in question is not underwritten by processes involving the manipulation of contents, nor is it, in itself, inherently contentful. Basic minds do not represent conditions that the world might be in. To think otherwise, as many do, is to ascribe features and characteristics to basic minds that belong only to encultured, scaffolded minds that are built atop them.

Just what is content? At its simplest, there is content wherever there are specified conditions of satisfaction. And there is true or accurate content wherever the conditions specified are, in fact, instantiated.

For many, it is definitional that minds—of any sort at all, including basic minds—entail the existence of content. Content, some hold, is necessitated by any intelligent interaction with the world. They take it that the best explanation of even the most basic kinds of cognition requires positing contents that are acquired and transformed in order to create representations that then inform and guide what an organism does or experiences. As we use the term, "basic cognition" means something narrower than "basic mentality." It denotes mental activity that exhibits intentional directedness, but it doesn't necessarily imply phenomenality. "Basic mentality" denotes mentality that may exhibit both intentional directedness and phenomenality.

It may be believed that wherever there is intentionally directed cognition there must be content in the sense defined above. To think this is to endorse an ambitious version of CIC, the thesis that Cognition necessarily Involves Content. More modestly, it may be believed that wherever there is at least perceptual experience there must be content. This would be to endorse a less ambitious version of CIC.

This book challenges the popular and deeply rooted intuition that at least one or other of these versions of CIC is true. We advance the fortunes of the counter-thesis: that there can be intentionally directed cognition and, even, perceptual experience without content. We maintain that this thesis may be true, and we try to make the reader believe it too. Not only is it not ruled out *a priori*; on close inspection, we find no compelling reasons to doubt its truth. Quite the opposite. As philosophers, we are in the business of promoting possibilities. We will have succeeded if, having reached the end of the book, the reader is convinced that the idea of contentless basic minds cannot be cursorily dismissed; that it is a live option that deserves to be taken much more seriously than it is currently.

Our game plan is to achieve this by radicalizing enactivism. *Radicalizing enactivism?!* Surely, enactivism is already quite radical enough! Enactivism, after all, gives explanatory pride of place to dynamic interactions between organisms and features of their environments over the contentful representation of such environmental features.

Many present-day philosophers and cognitive scientists acknowledge the importance of situated, environment-involving embodied engagements as a means of understanding basic minds. Yet despite being daring and groundbreaking in many respects, most existing enactive and embodied proposals about cognition are advanced in theoretically modest forms, often retaining some residual commitment to CIC. This commitment usually takes the form of holding fast to the view that basic minds are contentful but allowing that the vehicles that bear such contents—those at the coal face of cognitive processing—might be extra-neural, stretching into the wider body or the environment, at least in some instances. This is to endorse a form of Conservative Enactive or Embodied Cognition (abbreviated CEC).

By our lights, CEC doesn't go nearly far enough for its own good. In chapter 2 we will explain why, focusing on a prominent example. In a nutshell, it is only by completely rejecting CIC about basic minds that enactivism gains the resources for justifiably silencing its critics. If we are right, radicalizing enactivism is necessary if enactivism is to provide a stable, defensible, and strategically tenable framework for thinking about basic minds. This requires nothing short of a thoroughgoing and wholehearted rejection of CIC. Since certain prominent variants of enactivism harbor conservative tendencies and thus fail to break with tradition in the required way, it is necessary to press for a radicalized enactivism—that is, for Radical Enactive (or Embodied) Cognition (REC), which denies that basic minds are contentful.

Isn't this just riding the crest of a fashionable wave? It is certainly true that the widespread acceptance of embodied and enactive approaches in the cognitive sciences has anteceded a clear articulation and philosophical defense of such approaches—one that would motivate rational acceptance of their framework commitments. A convincing justification for believing in such approaches has lagged behind their general endorsement by the cognitive science community. This raises the worry that the whole enactive and embodied turn in cognitive science is backed by little or nothing more than an unreasoned attachment to certain attractive but ultimately empty pictures and slogans. For this reason, Prinz is right to proclaim that—at least in one sense—enactive and embodied approaches may be easier to "sell than to prove" (2009, p. 419).

We aim to supply the philosophical clarifications and strong support that have been sorely missing. In view of this ambition, we recognize that, in another sense, Prinz is quite wrong about REC's being an easy sell. Even when REC is backed by solid philosophical arguments that favor it, we don't expect that it will be attractive to many analytic philosophers. As things stand, there is great resistance even to the mere suggestion that the prominent forms of basic mentality of the sort that we discuss (which include human visual experience) might lack content. To many this is counterintuitive and plainly false.

We think REC has a better chance of being true than its CIC or CEC rivals. But we have to work hard to show this. We are well aware that some readers will be tempted to dismiss the view we favor as a non-starter. Worse, some will regard it as simply inconceivable. Thus, we concentrate our efforts on ensuring that REC gets a fair hearing. This is best done by testing its mettle against the best proposals of those who represent avant-garde thinking in the philosophy of cognitive science. In order of appearance, we critically review how it fares in comparison with claims made by Noë, Thompson, Clark, Wheeler, Dretske, Millikan, Gauker, Burge, Chalmers, McDowell, Menary, and Block.

Chapter 1 sets the stage for this labor, describing the revolutionary atmosphere of today's cognitive science, clarifying the pivotal theses on which REC leans, and introducing the main players—traditional CIC, newly articulated CEC, and REC—in more detail. Rather than trying to argue for REC straightaway, it prepares readers for that task, asking them to flex their imaginative muscles by first picturing how things would have to look if REC were true—and, by comparison, where REC lives in conceptual space.

Chapters 3–6 make a two-phase argument for REC. These chapters upset several bedrock assumptions about the nature of basic minds—assumptions that many regard to be, if not utterly beyond question, at least wholly secure and needing little attention.

Chapter 3 overturns the CIC applecart by examining familiar reasons for thinking that we can go at least part of the way toward explaining basic cognition without having to call on the notion of content at all. For example, the well-known successes in building flexible, behavior-based robots and understanding the environment-involving cognitive antics of certain insects appear to have progressed precisely because CIC thinking was rejected. Appealing to these developments, we argue that there is every reason to think the same approach will work when it comes to explaining many sophisticated human doings too— especially those associated with manual activities such as reaching and grasping. If this is right, it is possible that cognitive science may go much further than is typically supposed without CIC; potentially REC has real reach. This overcomes a familiar worry that REC, even if it is true in some domains, has a very limited scope.

Three main options present themselves to defenders of CIC at this point. Option A: These aren't cases involving bona fide cognition. The activities in question are too simple and directly coupled to the environment to require genuine cognitive explanation. This looks like mere *post hoc, ad hoc* stipulation. Option B: These are cases of bona fide cognition. REC is true of them. But cognition of this kind is extraordinarily limited. It won't "scale up" greatly, and hence it poses no interesting challenge to CIC's larger ambitions. Option C: These are cases of bona fide cognition. But they imply CIC—although the most promising CIC proposal about such cases comes in the form of CEC. Ergo, REC is false across the board.

Obviously, option C is the strongest, least concessionary move for fans of CIC to make. In considering whether such cognition really involves content, we describe the features of the most credible CEC challenge to REC, one that invokes action-oriented representations. In answer to this challenge, chapter 4 ups the ante and goes beyond the arguments provided in chapter 3 that were designed only to establish that we "don't need" CIC to explain many forms of basic cognitive activity. It argues that we simply "can't have" CIC accounts in this domain—even in the form of CEC—without surrendering explanatory naturalism.

All CIC accounts of basic cognition face a crippling problem: they are unable to account for the origins of content in the world if they are forced to use nothing but the standard naturalist resources of informational covariance, even if these are augmented by devices that have the biological function of responding to such information.

Defenders of CIC must face up to the Hard Problem of Content: that positing informational content is incompatible with explanatory naturalism. The root trouble is that Covariance doesn't Constitute Content. If covariance is the only scientifically respectable notion of information that can do the work required by explanatory naturalists, it follows that informational content doesn't exist in nature—or at least that it doesn't exist independently from and prior to the existence of certain social practices. If informational content doesn't exist in nature, then cognitive systems don't literally traffic in informational content, as CIC and CEC stories assume they do. This is so *a fortiori* if there is no naturally occurring informational content in the world.

The Hard Problem of Content presents proponents of CIC with a dilemma, and with the customary three possible moves. First, they might try to avoid the dilemma's horns by demonstrating that Covariance does Constitute Content, by showing that what they propose is already consistent with explanatory naturalism after all, or by finding another naturalistic candidate to explain informational content. We examine these possibilities but regard them to be forlorn. Second, they can opt to be impaled on the first horn: to posit informational content but reject explanatory naturalism. This might take the form of assuming that facts (including correspondences between facts) entail truth-bearing contents. This might work if contents were identical with their own truth conditions—that is, if they somehow both specified and realized their conditions of satisfaction in absence of thinkers. Accordingly, informational contents might be primitive, unexplained features of reality itself. However, there is a price, since it is not obvious that this proposal is compatible with physicalism. Still, it might be compatible with some kind of unexplanatory naturalism. For example, informational content might be an irreducible property of fundamental reality, having status similar to that of qualia in Chalmers' system. Third, they can opt to be impaled on the second horn. This looks less painful. It requires accepting that covariance doesn't entail or constitute content—i.e., that it lacks inherent, truth-bearing properties. But it also requires accepting that the only scientifically respectable notion of information in play—the only one that can do the work required by naturalists—is the notion of information as covariance. However, if this is accepted it follows that sensitivity to covariances is not sensitivity to informational content.

Adopting this third option assumes that basic cognition boils down to systems engaging in informationally sensitive interactions with environmental offerings. This involves being sensitive to covariant information, but it doesn't involve picking up and processing informational contents. Cognitive systems don't "pick up" or "take in" any informational contents; there are no such things as informational contents to take in. Such imagined contents are not "objective commodities," and cognitive systems do not "traffic" in them in the ways CIC and CEC require.

At this point, the best and most strategically secure move that friends of CIC can make is to cut their losses by surrendering the idea that content is needed in order to explain the kinds of engaged activity that have been the focus of attention up to this point. Their retreat might take the form either of a concession to REC or of a revival of the Option A strategy (that of denying that the activity in question implies bona fide cognition). Either way, CICers of this persuasion insist that content comes into play only when there are quite distinctive mental phenomena to be accounted for. With this in mind, it turns out that there are good reasons to try to draw the CIC line when what is being dealt with is full-blown perception and perceptual experience. *Prima facie*, it looks to be a good bet that where we find mentality of this kind we—undeniably—find the most basic, truly contentful minds.

Chapter 5 lays out the options for those who plan to fall back on perception, invoking this strategy to preserve CIC. In particular, it reveals why adopting a hyperintellectualist position is of no avail. Apart from assuming that perceptual experience is inherently contentful, hyperintellectualists also assume that it depends on a great deal of background representational activity. These latter commitments inherit the problems of the discredited CIC accounts—those examined and dismissed in chapter 4. Nevertheless, all of the commitments that make hyperintellectualism "hyper" can be rejected in favor of a minimal intellectualism—one that skirts the crippling Hard Problem of Content while remaining a solid CIC proposal about perceptual experience. We consider how those who want to defend CIC in this domain might go even lower, adopting maximally minimal intellectualism—the most modest and credible CIC view of how perceptual experience might be essentially contentfully representational.

The preceding analysis sets the stage for CIC's last stand. Having clarified these matters, we are able to assess whether REC might not plausibly advance further into what is generally taken to be utterly safe CIC territory, extending its reach to include perceptual experience—even human visual experience. To show that such an advance is plausible, chapter 6 argues against the best and most plausible maximally minimal intellectualist proposals on today's market. After detailed examination, it is found—in the cold light of reason—that those proposals offer no serious resistance, and that there is no compelling ground for rejecting the conclusion that perceptual experience is inherently contentless.

Let us be clear. In pressing for REC, we do not say that CIC is never true. We do not say that cognition is never informed by or never involves content. We have no truck with that claim. We are not advancing *Really* Radical Enactive or Embodied Cognition as a thesis about the nature of *all* minds. Some cognitive activity—plausibly, that associated with and dependent upon the mastery of language—surely involves content. Still, if our analyses are right, a surprising amount of mental life (including some canonical forms of it, such as human visual experience) may well be inherently contentless. If true this is not trivial, since such forms are often taken to definitively imply the existence of representational content. If REC is true, then CIC's picture of basic minds must be surrendered completely. This picture of mind to be abandoned has dominated mainstream philosophical and scientific thinking, in one way or another, since the days of Descartes, Hobbes, and Locke.

Some interesting results follow from trading in CIC, even in the form of CEC, for REC. In chapter 7 we examine what acceptance of REC means for the now stagnating debate about the extent and boundaries of mind. We argue that—at least, with respect to their intentional aspects—basic minds are extensive and not merely extended if they are contentless. We demonstrate how REC decisively advances debates about whether minds extend, moving beyond traditional stalemates. We show how it is possible to refurbish some of the best proposals that have come forth from these discussions if REC is accepted. Specifically, we argue that thinking on this topic must be reframed in terms of extensive but contentless basic minds. We show that it is possible that basic minds might be transformed, through engaging in wider practices, to become contentful scaffolded minds.

In chapter 8, we consider REC's implications for thinking about phenomenal consciousness. Does REC imply the conclusions about the extent of phenomenality that many enactivists argue for? Is there any compelling reason to suppose that phenomenality is extensive? The answers are complex. We use this chapter as an opportunity to correct some understandable confusions about the exact value of the enactivist strategy of going wide and looking to environmental features when explaining why the phenomenal characters of experiences are as they are. The strategy of going wide is often thought to be a hopeless attempt to directly solve the Hard Problem of Consciousness. We argue that going wide has a different, subtler explanatory function. Moreover, the explanatory value of this move is not undermined, even if it is accepted that the supervenience basis of phenomenality is wholly brain-bound.

As a finale, we show that understanding phenomenal consciousness as activity and consideration of its actual and natural origins gives us the resources to deal with the Hard Problem of Consciousness. We do not attempt to provide a straight solution to the Hard Problem of Consciousness (something we regard as impossible); rather, we aim to motivate belief in relevant identities that obviate the need to solve it.

Ultimately, our purpose in advancing REC is, in a sense, polit-ical. Like Noë (2009, p. xiv), we aim "to change the world [or] at least to shake up the cognitive science establishment." We intend to show that, at least in this case, Prinz (2009, p. 419) is wrong to hold that "radicalism may be good for politics, but it's bad for science."

This short book is really an enactivist manifesto—an argu-mentative one in the service of science. It presses for REC by articulating considerations that make it clear that REC is not only possibly true but in fact a good bet. At the very least, we hope to expose that, although CIC enjoys the status of the default view in some circles, there is reason to kick the CIC habit when it comes to thinking about basic minds. CIC-ish thinking in this domain is much more rickety than is typically supposed, and rival REC proposals, though radical, are not reckless.

Acknowledgments

First and foremost we wish to acknowledge the tolerant patience of our wives—Farah Hutto and Inez Germeys—and children—Alexander, Justin, and Emerson, the three Hutto boys, and Elise, Charlotte, and Laure, the three Myin girls. A great deal of family time was lost during our collaboration, and we both spent more time away from home than we, or our families, would have wished.

We are especially grateful to the Fonds voor Wetenschappelijk Onderzoek-Vlaanderen (Research Foundation Flanders), the Research Council of the University of Antwerp, and the University of Hertfordshire for directly funding our collaborations as co-authors. Erik Myin drew support from the Fonds voor Wetenschappelijk Onderzoek-Vlaanderen by means of the Research Grant "Radical Enactivism" (1.5.207.09.N.00), a Sabbatical Leave Grant covering the months from September 2011 to February 2012, as well as through the projects "Senses as Tools" (G.0.321.09.N.10) and "Computation Reconsidered" (G0B5312N). The Research Council of the University of Antwerp generously funded the Small Project "Consciousness Clarified" and the New Research Initiative "Imagery as Perceptual Activity." Dan Hutto also thanks the Australian Research Council Discovery Project, "Embodied Virtues and Expertise" (DP: 1095109); the Marie-Curie Initial Training Network, "TESIS: Towards an

Embodied Science of InterSubjectivity" (FP7-PEOPLE-2010-ITN, 264828); and the (Ministerio de Economía e innovación) Spanish Department of Economy and Innovation: "Agency, Normativity and Identity: the Presence of the Subject in Actions" (FFI-2011-25131) for support that made other regular international activities and visits possible.

We are grateful to the staff members of the Elzenveld Centrum in Antwerp, the Pennyfarthing Hotel in Berkhamsted, and the Hôtel du Panthéon in Paris for their kind services while housing us over the years. We especially thank the latter for allowing two philosophers to feature as part of the lobby décor during the last days of finishing the book.

For their insightful comments, challenges, and other intellectual stimuli along the way we thank Kristin Andrews, Malika Auvray, Tim Bayne, Tony Chemero, Sam Coleman, Ed Cooke, Ron Chrisley, Andy Clark, Daniel Dennett, Shaun Gallagher, Vittorio Gallese, Christopher Gauker, the late Susan Hurley, Pierre Jacob, Fred Keijzer, Steven Laurence, Richard Menary, Danièle Moyal-Sharrock, Bence Nanay, Alva Noë, Kevin O'Regan, Jesse Prinz, John Searle, Corrado Sinigaglia, Marc Slors, Pierre Steiner, and Mike Wheeler.

We thank our colleagues and PhD students Lars De Nul, Jan Degenaar, Bas Donders, Joanna Gillies, Geert Gooskens, Victor Loughlin, Peter Reynaert, Joachim Leilich, Zuzanna Rucinska, Johan Veldeman, and Karim Zahidi for providing an enjoyable and stimulating work environment. Bas Donders, Jan Degenaar, and Joanna Gillies deserve additional acknowlegment for proofreading the manuscript during various stages of its preparation.

We are grateful to the organizers of the many events at which we have been invited to present work. We would like to thank the organizers and audiences of events that took place at the following venues for having provided opportunities to clarify and develop ideas: Sheffield, November 2011; Philosophy of Neurosciences Workshop, Louvain la Neuve, November 2011; School of Visual Arts, New York, October 2011; Ecap7, Milan, September 2011; Swedish Graduate Summer School for Cognitive Science (SweCog), August 2011; Arcus Foundation, New York, August 2011; International conference on Memory, York, August 2011; Royal College of Arts, London, June 2011; Extended Cognition Workshop; University of Amsterdam, June 2011; Free University of Amsterdam, May 2011; King's College, London, April 2011; Berlin School of Mind and Brain, Zentrum für Kulturforschung and Collegium for Advanced Studies, October 2010; Third Workshop on the Philosophy of Information, November 2010, Brussels; Institute of Cognitive Science, University of Osnabrück, October 2010; University of Sydney, December 2009, VAF IV, Louvain, January 2010; University of Wollongong, November 2009; Humboldt-University Berlin, November 2009; Clark Centennial Conference, Worcester, Massachusetts, October 2009; ESF workshop on Neuroesthetics, Milan, September 2009; University of Milan, May 2009; Dubrovnik, April 2009; Universidad de Sevilla, February 2009; University of Heidelberg, Sept 2008; Fondazione Rosselli, Turin, September 2008; University of Antwerp, September 2008; University of Central Florida, Orlando, October 2007; Brain and Mind Forum, Helsinge, Denmark, August 2007; Jean Piaget Society, Amsterdam, May 2007; Nicholaus Copernicus University, Torun, November 2006; Ecole Normale Supérieure, Lyon, November 2006; ASSC10, Oxford, June 2006; Central Division of the American Philosophical Association, Chicago, December 2005.

We are grateful to the editors and publishers of the following for allowing the reuse of some material in chapters 2–4 of this book:

"Radically enactive cognition in our grasp," in *The Hand—An Organ of the Mind*, ed. Z. Radman (MIT Press, forthcoming)

"Enactivism: Why be radical?" in *Sehen und Handeln*, ed. H. Bredekamp and J. M. Krois (Akademie Verlag, 2011)

"Philosophy of mind's new lease on life: Autopoietic enactivism meets teleosemiotics," *Journal of Consciousness Studies* 18 (2011), no. 5–6, 44–64

"Truly enactive emotion," *Emotion Review* 4 (2012), no. 2, 176–181.

Last but far from least, we are grateful to the people at the MIT Press with whom we had the opportunity to cooperate in bringing this Fodor-weight manifesto into being: Philip Laughlin, our editor, for his patience and cheerful support in all matters, and Paul Bethge, for his excellent copy editing.

Abbreviations

CIC	Content Involving Cognition
CEC	Conservative Enactive (or Embodied) Cognition
cEMH	complementarity-motivated Extended Mind Hypothesis
DEUTS	Dynamical Entanglement plus Unique Temporal Signature
DIM	Default Internal Mind
EMH	Extended Mind Hypothesis
pEMH	parity-motivated Extended Mind Hypothesis
REC	Radical Enactive (or Embodied) Cognition

1 Enactivism: The Radical Line

Heresies are experiments in man's unsatisfied search for truth.
—H. G. Wells

The Specter of Enactivism

For those working in the sciences of the mind, these are interesting times. Revolution is, yet again, in the air. This time it has come in the wake of *avant-garde* Enactive or Embodied approaches to cognition that bid us to reform our thinking about the basic nature of mind. Today, "embodied cognition is sweeping the planet" (Adams 2010, p. 619). The most radical versions of these approaches are marked by their uncompromising and thoroughgoing rejection of intellectualism about the basic nature of mind, abandoning the idea that all mentality involves or implies content. Call this—the view we defend—Radically Enactive (or Embodied) Cognition—REC for short.

Influenced by phenomenology, dynamical systems theory, and developments in robotics, proponents of Enactive and Embodied ways of thinking reject the familiar explanatory framework of orthodox cognitive science in favor of alternative platforms. Adherents of such views deny that the best way to explain cognition is to posit the construction of internal representational models built on the basis of retrieved informational content. Chemero (2009, p. 77) captures the spirit of this turn with particular reference to dynamical systems:

[T]he representational description of the system does not add much to our understanding. . . . [Thus,] despite the fact that one can cook up a representational story once one has the dynamical explanation, the representational gloss does not predict anything about the system's behavior that could not be predicted by dynamical explanation alone.

Enactive and embodied approaches have proved popular and fruitful; yielding a great variety of proposals about many topics, including perception, intentionality, emotion, memory, social cognition, and consciousness. (For an overview, see Robbins and Aydede 2009.) These proposals are refreshing in that they either fully reject the long-established paradigm in cognitive science or, at least, abandon some of its starting assumptions. Unlike the rank and file in orthodox philosophy of mind and cognitive science, followers of the new movement question—in ways more or less radical—the presumed divide between what is mindless, mechanical, dispositional, and behavioral and what is properly mental, representational, intentional, and phenomenal.

Reporting on these developments, Ramsey observes that "something very interesting is taking place in cognitive science. . . . Cognitive science has taken a dramatic anti-representational turn" (2007, pp. xiv–xv). The importance of this challenge is not lost on those at the center of the action. Not since the ousting of behaviorism (at the advent of the most recent cognitive revolution) has there been such a root-and-branch challenge to widely accepted assumptions about the very nature of basic minds. In a remarkable reversal of fortune, it is now a live question to what extent, if any, representational and computational theories of the mind and cognition—those that have dominated for so long—ought to play a fundamental role in our explanatory framework for understanding intelligent activity. Defenders of REC argue that the usual suspects—representation and computation—are not definitive of, and do not form the basis of, all mentality.

In light of the pace at which things have progressed, interested onlookers viewing matters from the sidelines might be forgiven for thinking the revolution is already over. Enactive and Embodied ways of thinking about mind and cognition are certainly already comfortably ensconced in cognitive science, having established deep roots in a number of disciplines. Far from merely being at the gates, the barbarians are, it seems, now occupying cafés and wine bars in the heart of the city.

Even those who most regret this development are prepared to acknowledge that there has been a sea change. Lamenting the rise of a pragmatist trend in cognitive science, Fodor (2008b) acknowledges that this new style of thinking in cognitive science is now in the mainstream. He puts this down to an infectious disease of thought ("a bad cold," as he puts it on page 10). Others are edgily aware of the specter of Enactive and Embodied approaches "haunting the laboratories of cognitive science" (Goldman and de Vignemont 2009, p. 154). "Pervasive and unwelcome" is the verdict of these authors: commitment to such approaches may be everywhere, but this is something to be cured or exorcised as soon as possible.

Despite their increase in popularity, which some hope is nothing more than a short-lived trend, the legitimacy of these revolutionary approaches remains hotly contested. It is certainly true that there hasn't yet been a definitive articulation of the central and unifying assumptions of such approaches. Indeed, there is some reason to doubt that it will be possible to group together all of the offerings that nominally travel under the banner of Enactive and Embodied cognition by identifying their commitment to a set of well-defined theoretical tenets. (See Shapiro 2011, p. 3.) Neither Enactive Cognition nor Embodied Cognition is a label for a well-defined theory of the mind; rather, Enactive Cognition and Embodied Cognition denote broad frameworks for understanding the basic nature of minds and how they become more elaborate.

Enactivism RECtified

Enactivism is inspired by the insight that the embedded and embodied activity of living beings provides the right model for understanding minds.[1] To understand mentality, however complex and sophisticated it may be, it is necessary to appreciate how living beings dynamically interact with their environments: ultimately, there is no prospect of understanding minds without reference to interactions between organisms and their environments.

When first explicating the idea that mind is best conceived as a kind of embodied action, the founders of enactivism, Francisco Varela, Evan Thompson, and Eleanor Rosch, defined embodiment in terms of an organism's various sensorimotor capacities—capacities embedded in and engaged with wider contexts of the biological, psychological, and cultural varieties. In emphasizing the essential link between mentality and embodied and embedded activity, the express aim of the original version of enactivism was to oppose and serve as an antidote to those approaches to mind that "take representation as their central notion" (Varela, Thompson, and Rosch 1991, p. 172).

Organismic activity—engaging with features of their environments in specifiable ways—suffices for the most basic kinds of cognition. Such activity does not depend upon individuals retrieving informational content from the world—content that is then processed and manipulated—in order to attribute properties to the world. In short, not all mentality requires individuals to construct representations of their worlds. This is REC—the position we defend in this book.

Not all contemporary spokespersons for enactivism are as steadfast in their commitment to this anti-content, anti-representational view, as we show in chapter 2. Yet we intend to demonstrate that REC is the only truly tenable kind of enactivism. The only good enactivism is a properly radical enactivism.

In this book we remain neutral toward other, more extravagant claims associated with the original version of enactivism. Certainly they are not implied by, and play no role in, our anti-content arguments. Most prominent among such ideas is the thought that organisms "enact" or "bring forth" their worlds— that enaction enables a world to "show up" for individuals. This, it is claimed, holds true not only for simple creatures but also, and equally, for humans. Some pioneering enactivists hold that "our perceived world" (that is, the world as perceived) is "*constituted* through complex and delicate patterns of sensorimotor activity" (Varela, Thompson, and Rosch 1991, p. 164, emphasis added).

Our concern here is not to advance or defend all of the ideas associated with enactivism. We restrict our ambitions to promoting REC, calling upon strong versions of two theses. We dub these the Embodiment Thesis and the Developmental-Explanatory Thesis. The former equates basic cognition with concrete spatio-temporally extended patterns of dynamic interaction between organisms and their environments. To understand this claim aright, it is important to recall that, for enactivists, embodiment is not defined with reference to an intuitive, every-day understanding of bodies and their boundaries, but in terms of wide-reaching organismic sensorimotor interactions that are contextually embedded.[2] These interactions are assumed to take the form of activity that unfolds across time and which essentially involves individuals engaging with aspects of their environments.

Enactivists hold that these dynamic interactions—in which cognition literally consists—are loopy, not linear. For example, in ordinary cases perceptual experience is made possible by organisms engaging with select aspects of the environment in a continuous series of responses that call into play the non-neural body and many areas of the brain. These neural and wider bodily responses are influenced by activity that involves non-trivial causal spread within the brain and the body and among the brain, the body, and the environment. Multiple areas in the brain and the body are involved in processes of mutual and concurrent interaction, and patterns of simultaneous recipro-cal causation occur among the environment, the brain, and the body.

Variables in the environment influence and are influenced by variables in the brain and the non-neural body in a recurrent manner, making it impossible to conceive of these as linear rela-tions holding between inputs and outputs. Clark (2009, p. 975) wryly characterizes this series of ongoing looping interactions as "Escher Spaghetti." From the vantage point of dynamical systems theory, there is no way to isolate properly mentality-constituting "inner" organismic responses from "outer" ones that allegedly stand over and against the former as mere causal contributions from the environment. On this model, there is no prospect of making any such principled division.

That said, for enactivists dynamical systems theory only provides a convenient platform for a new philosophical framework for thinking about the basic nature of mind. Enactivists leave to others the work of deciding exactly which set of complex temporally extended and spatially extensive dynamical responses are minimally necessary for the occurrence of this or that kind of cognition. In deciding those issues, the devil is, as ever, in the empirical details. Adherents of the strong Embodiment Thesis assume that, no matter how the empirical questions are answered, mentality—with the possible exception of phenomenality, as we discuss in chapter 8—is in *all* cases concretely constituted by, and thus literally consists in, the extensive ways in which organisms interact with their environments, where the relevant ways of interacting involve, but are not exclusively restricted to, what goes on in brains.

Accordingly, what is distinctive about REC is its commitment to the idea that cognition is essentially extensive and not merely, as Clark and Chalmers (1998) famously argued, extended— a view we defend in chapter 7. The difference between these claims is that the Extended Mind Hypothesis (EMH) doesn't rule out the assumption that biologically basic cognition is, by default, brain-bound. Thus, prominent versions of EMH assume that only in exceptional cases—for example, when non-bodily add-ons are required in order to make the achievement of certain cognitive tasks possible—do minds extend. By contrast, those who endorse REC and thus the strongest version of the Embodiment Thesis assume that minds are already, in their basic nature, extensive and wide-ranging.

Some enactivists take the strong Embodiment Thesis to be true not only of paradigmatically mental and cognitive states of mind (as defenders of the REC would have it) but also of the phenomenal aspects of conscious experiences. (See Noë 2009.) Though we do not endorse this view, we agree with such enactivists that the phenomenal properties of experience— what-it-is-like properties—should not be identified with extra ingredients over and above the dynamic, interactive responses of organisms.

No concessions are made to those who believe in qualia and who think there is something more to be explained. Radical enactivists hold that phenomenality is nothing other than speci-fiable sorts of activity—even if only neural activity—and is not to be identified with additional items of mental acquaintance. Yet, although we allow that the minimal supervenience basis for phenomenality might be narrow, we hold that to understand phenomenal experience fully unavoidably requires attending to the original, environment-involving ways in which individuals engage with certain worldly offerings through bouts of extended sensorimotor interaction.

REC is also committed to the Developmental-Explanatory Thesis, which holds that mentality-constituting interactions are grounded in, shaped by, and explained by nothing more, or other, than the history of an organism's previous interactions. Sentience and sapience emerge through repeated processes of organismic engagement with environmental offerings. For organisms capable of learning, it is this, and nothing else, that determines which aspects of their worlds are significant to them. Nothing other than its history of active engaging structures or explains an organism's current interactive tendencies. Fodor (2008b, p. 10) is thus right to observe that the sort of approach enactivists promote insists that "abilities are prior to theories," that "competence is prior to content," and that "knowing how is the paradigm cognitive state and it is prior to knowing that."

A prolonged history of interactive encounters is the basis of creatures' current embodied tendencies, know-how, and skills. To invoke the favorite poetic motto of enactivists, this is essentially a process of "laying down a path in walking."[3] The secret to explaining what structures an organism's current mental activity lies entirely in its history of previous engagements and not in some set of internally stored mental rules and representations.

CIC, REC, and CEC

A tradition of thinking about the nature of mind that is alive and well in many quarters of Anglophone philosophy of mind and cognitive science takes it for granted that "the manipulation and use of representations is the primary job of the mind" (Dretske 1995, p. xiv). If representations are thought to be necessarily contentful, this entails a commitment to Content Involving Cognition (CIC), which defines intellectualism.

CIC assumes that cognition requires the existence of contents of some kind or other. Unrestricted CIC takes this to be true of all mentality, always and everywhere. Its intellectualist credo is "no mentality without content."[4] As we have already noted, for the staunchest backers of CIC the widespread influence of the enactive turn and of the associated ideas that minds are Embodied, Embedded, and Extensive is perceived as unwelcome, faddish, unfortunate, and retrograde.

The idea that mentality is Enactive and Embodied poses a challenge to unrestricted CIC only if advanced in an uncompromisingly radical version, such as REC—a version that rejects all vestiges of the idea that basic mentality is necessarily contentful. For there are ways of acknowledging that mentality is supported by Enactive and Embodied means that are wholly compatible with, and quite acceptable, even to unrestricted CIC. For example, its intellectualist proponents can happily accept that various facts about embodiment are causally necessary in making mentality possible and shaping its character without this concession threatening the idea that mentality is wholly constituted by representational or contentful facts or properties.

For example, it is clearly true that what a creature perceives depends on contingent facts about the nature of its sensory apparatus—that bats, dolphins, and rattlesnakes perceive the world differently and perceive different things because they are differently embodied. No one denies that what and how we perceive causally depends on what we do—that it is only because I move my eyes and my head in certain ways that certain things become visible and audible.

If this is all that proponents of Enactive and Embodied approaches to cognition are claiming, their contributions in no way threaten even the most ambitious version of CIC. Indeed, this hardly goes beyond stating the trivially obvious. Some enactivists make statements that encourage such weak readings. For example, with respect to the Embodiment Thesis, Varela, Thompson, and Rosch occasionally talk in ways that suggest that they are committed only to anodyne claims about determination relations—claims that can be easily read in terms that imply nothing more than causal dependence. For example, they write that "the manner in which the perceiver is embodied . . . determines how the perceiver can act and be modulated by environmental events" (1991, p. 173).

A more interesting and challenging version of the Embodiment Thesis that several authors have independently settled upon advances the idea that extended bodily states and processes might serve as representational or information-carrying vehicles that play unique computational roles in enabling some forms of cognition (Clark 2008a). Alternatively, in the lingo of Goldman and de Vignemont (2009), perhaps the most promising version of the Embodiment Thesis is that some mental representations are "encoded in essentially bodily formats." We take this to mean that for some kinds of cognition only a bodily vehicle will do. These renderings of the Embodiment Thesis allow one to recognize "the profound contributions that embodiment and embedding make" (Clark 2008a, p. 45). At the same time, they don't break faith with unrestricted CIC. If this is all that proponents of Enactive and Embodied approaches are offering, they may be, at most, supplying new tools or "welcome accessories" of considerable potential value that could augment intellectualist accounts of the mind.[5]

Those who take the more daring line of positing bodily vehicles (or essentially bodily vehicles—i.e., bodily formats) of content endorse only Conservative Enactive (or Embodied) Cognition (CEC). CEC does not break faith with unrestricted CIC. Though such conservative renderings are possible, they obviously go against the spirit of an enactivism that is serious about its rejection of content and representation. REC presses for the strongest reading of the Embodiment Thesis—one that uncompromisingly maintains that basic cognition is literally constituted by, and to be understood in terms of, concrete patterns of environmental situated organismic activity, nothing more or less.

Indeed, this radical reading gets both its substance and its mandate from a thoroughgoing rejection of CIC. If mentality is not at root content involving, there is no reason to suppose, even in principle, that it is possible to individuate and isolate some portion of organismic activity—a portion that falls short of an organism's total way of responding to some worldly offering—that can be identified with properly cognitive activity. Consequently, according to REC, there is no way to distinguish neural activity that is imagined to be genuinely content involving (and thus truly mental, truly cognitive) from other non-neural activity that merely plays a supporting or enabling role in making mind and cognition possible.

In other words, once one abandons the idea that mentality is essentially content involving there is no *a priori* reason to suppose that cognition is an exclusively heady affair. Rejection of CIC, and along with it representationalism, thus provides the cleanest and clearest motivation for thinking that cognition is fully embodied and embedded, and not merely embrained. This is the true hallmark of REC.

Unrestricted CIC and REC logically exclude one another. They are incompatible claims about the basic nature of mentality. Unrestricted CIC and REC can't live together. To borrow Fodor's (2008b) turn of phrase, they are enemies par excellence. Without some concessions on both sides, there is no way to square the circle and bring these views into friendly communion.

Still, it might be thought that there are good reasons for making such concessions—that it is wise for both parties to restrict their ambitions. Because this will be a prominent and recurring theme in chapters 3, 5, and 6, it is worth clarifying one important matter straightaway. Consider the Developmental-Explanatory Thesis. By giving pride of place to embodied habits and skills when it comes to explaining how sophisticated mentality emerges, REC denies CIC accounts of the same. REC's credo— that "we act before we think"—is an outright denial of the CIC thesis that "we must think in order to act."

Yet even the most radical of enactivists need not, and should not, deny the existence and importance of contentful and representationally based modes of thinking; it is just that these should be regarded as emerging late in phylogeny and ontogeny, being dependent on immersion in special sorts of shared practices.[6] (See Hutto 2008, chapter 6; see also Williams 2010, Gauker 2011.) Enactivists are concerned to defend the view that our most elementary ways of engaging with the world and others—including our basic forms of perception and perceptual experience—are mindful in the sense of being phenomenally charged and intentionally directed, despite being non-representational and content-free. Defending this understanding of basic mentality is the primary aim of this book.

What is ruled out by REC is that content-involving mentality is basic and is found in any and all forms of mindedness. Paul Churchland criticizes the latter view in the following passage:

In ascribing propositional attitudes to ourselves as our basic cognitive states, and explaining our behaviour in their terms, we are evidently trying to characterize . . . truly amazing cognitive [activity] in terms of exactly one parochial game that only one species of animal has recently learned to play: language. From this perspective, why should we suspect, even for a moment, that human language would reflect the basic elements and structure of . . . cognition? (2007, p. 180)

Once Churchland's assessement is modified to free it from unwarranted neurocentrism, proponents of REC can happily agree with it. Like classic eliminativism, REC denies that basic mentality and cognition should be modeled in terms of propositional attitudes. But unlike classical eliminativism, REC does not claim that propositional attitude explanations are never appropriate. REC holds that some organisms have more than one way of getting around cognitively, and that some organisms—language users, at least—are capable of genuinely contentful, representational modes of thinking and reasoning.

What REC insists on is that creatures are capable of dealing with aspects of their environments, sometimes in quite remarkable and sophisticated ways (ways that count as properly mental and cognitive), even if the capacity for content-involving deliberation or planning never develops. REC happily concedes that some very important forms of cognition essentially depend on the interactions between propositional attitudes. Thus, REC is compatible with a restricted CIC. To assume otherwise is to misunderstand REC's scope and interests.

Ambiguity about the notion of action can cause confusion on this score. Enactivists inspired by its original formulation invoke the notion of "embodied action" even when describing mental activity that doesn't involve content or representations of any kind. For intellectualists this makes no sense, since for them nothing qualifies as an action proper unless it is produced by or otherwise connected to contentful states of mind of some sort. Thus, when enactivists speak of "embodied action" and their intellectual opponents talk of "action," they are not operating with the same notion of action. There is a chance that when this semantic confusion is cleared up the relevant philosophical work might be divvied up so that REC and restricted CIC complement each other. But this envisaged rapprochement between REC and restricted CIC is not in the cards as long as intellectualist extremists continue to demand that a bout of activity counts as mindful only if it is connected with contentful states of mind. As long as that commitment is in place, CIC is unrestricted and logically excludes REC.

RECers assume that many sophisticated embodied engagements constitute mentality and are best explained with reference to nothing more than habits of mind, without the need to invoke the existence of any content-involving or representationally informed cognition whatsoever. But since many CICers are unwilling to concede even this, it turns out that deciding whether REC is true of basic mentality is a high-stakes business of real theoretical interest. At least with respect to basic cognition, REC has the potential to replace, and not merely complement, CIC. Hence, REC is nothing less than a fundamental rethinking of the very foundations of standard approaches to cognitive science and philosophy of mind.

A Walk on the Wild Side

Despite its revolutionary ambitions, REC starts in the same place as other familiar approaches to the mind. For example, it assumes that focusing on sensory stimulation isn't enough when it comes to understanding perceptual experience. Various considerations support this conclusion.

For one thing, it is arguable that the phenomenology of experience involves appreciating the perceptual presence of objects in the environment, but perception cannot be accounted for solely in terms of raw stimulation and perturbation of sensory modalities. Thus, the visual experience of a tomato as a three-dimensional object, taking up space voluminously, cannot be explained simply by appealing to what is, in old money, "given" to the senses. For what is, strictly, provided to the visual system is only—at most—a partial, two-dimensional take of the tomato.

Other, more purely empirical findings suggest the same—that there is a need to distinguish between sensing and experiencing. It has been shown to be possible to be sensorially stimulated in normal ways without being able to experience features or

aspects of the surrounding environment in genuinely perceptual ways—that is, in ways that allow for competent engagements with worldly offerings and/or that enable one to make
genuinely perceptual reports. This is the situation, for example,
of post-operative cataract patients and of people first learning
to manipulate sensory substitution devices (O'Regan and Noë
2001; Noë 2004).

In addition, there is neuroscientific evidence that points this
way. Freeman, who recorded EEG patterns during rabbit olfac-
tion, revealed that "the patterns of response of the bulb to a
given stimulus have a lot more to do with the state of the bulb
than they do with the actual sensory activity evoked by the stimulus," and that hence "activity on the sensory surfaces cannot
strongly determine the activity of the bulb" (1991, p. 78).

Thus, there are good philosophical and empirical reasons
for thinking that something must be added to sensory stimulation to yield full-blown experience of worldly offerings, and
to enable organisms to engage with them successfully. This is
widely agreed. But there are very different stories about what
exactly is added that makes the crucial difference.

CIC-ish intellectualists propose that a conceptual template or
representational schema of some kind has to be brought into
play, and that it is the application of concepts or representations
to sensory contents that converts merely sensational informational content into representational content proper. This, they
claim, does the trick of yielding contents that say how things
stand in the world of the experience. (See, e.g., Fodor 2008b.)
This idea is much in evidence in Marr's famous computational
theory of vision: his account of how information in two-dimensional arrays of stimulation on the retina is converted into a
representation of the three-dimensional world as containing a

distribution of colored and moving objects in space. (See Marr 1982.)

Like certain other enactivist approaches, REC rejects the idea that the exercise of conceptual or representational capacities is needed and instead looks to the history of organismic activity as providing the something extra. Thus, what is necessary for experiencing, in addition to appropriate sensory stimulation, is the organism's history and embodied habits of interacting.

Enactivists offer a gradual and variegated story of how organisms become able to respond to and engage with relevant features of their environments in cognitively sensitive and sophisticated ways, ranging from more basic forms of experiencing to more genuinely symbol-based thinking.

The elephant in the room is, of course, the standard charge that any enactivism that rejects representationalism—and hence cognitivism—in an uncompromising manner must reduce to some kind of behaviorism. This association springs readily to mind. Certainly, as Ramsey (2007, p. xv) suggests, if it turns out that "many current cognitive theories are . . . not actually representational theories, then we need to reconsider the scope of the so-called 'cognitive revolution' and the degree to which modern cognitivism is really so different from certain forms of behaviorism." So does REC leave itself open to being justifiably accused of being, as ecological psychology has been, merely a form of "dressed-up behaviorism" (Shapiro 2011, p. 38)?

Despite the popularity of this sort of automatic assimilation, non-representationalist teleofunctionalism is a closer theoretical analog to REC. Standard teleofunctionalism appeals to the notion of organismic proper (or teleo-) functions—those that are defined in terms of the ends they serve for organisms. These functions are not to be confused with purely systemic functions of the sort that are defined by the role an item or device plays within a more complex system. Rather, they concern what a device or an item is supposed to do, as opposed to what it is disposed to do.

In explicating teleofunctions, a familiar naturalist strategy is to appeal to a principled notion of biological function. This has the alleged advantage of allowing teleofunctionalists to account for the basis and the source of the norms in question without violating explanatory naturalism. There are a number of ways of doing this, but by far the most popular has been to explain the basis of the norms etiologically—that is, by appealing to the historical conditions and evolutionary pressures under which the devices were forged.

Construed thus, proper functions are explained in terms of normal conditions of operation that tell how a function was historically performed on those (perhaps rare) occasions when it was properly performed. The historical conditions in question are those in which a given biological response originally conferred the sort of benefits that brought about, or contributed to, the selection of its underlying mechanism. Appeal to historically normal conditions therefore makes it possible to explain why a device, an entity, or a response proliferated. That, in turn, enables us to say what it is supposed to be doing, even in cases in which it fails to achieve its ends. Using these conceptual tools, some have tried to provide a naturalized representational theory of content, focusing on the use that is made of purported inner states in order to achieve specific organismic ends or purposes.

The link between REC and a modified teleofunctionalism becomes evident, for example, if we take Dretske's representational account of experience and give it an important, albeit partial, makeover. Dretske, a stalwart supporter of unrestricted

CIC, regards all mental facts as representational facts. He even defends the view that "experience is a special kind of representation—a nonconceptual form of representation" (1995, p. 1). His account of representation is as follows: "The fundamental idea is that a system, S, represents a property, F, if and only if S has the function of indicating (providing information about) the F of a certain domain of objects." (ibid., p. 2) Dretske thus understands representation in a two-tiered fashion, combining teleological and information-theoretic ideas. He is inclined to endorse representationalism about experience, at least in part, because he believes it is necessary if we are to explain the intentional properties of experience.

We have provided only the bare bones of Dretske's account and its motivations, because at this stage we are interested only in seeing what happens if we throw out his commitment to representationalism and keep the rest of his theory. To logically transform Dretske's theory along the proposed lines is to let go of the idea that experiences represent situations in contentful ways. This requires giving up the idea that, in the right conditions, my seeing red represents the presence of redness truly or accurately.

Yet if we give up this representationalist commitment, what is left? Behaviorism? No. What is left is much of the basic apparatus of teleofunctionalism minus the idea that experiences have the function of "saying," "indicating," " or "representing." The teleofunctional approach is revised to assert, much more modestly than Dretske's variant, that experiencing organisms are set up to be set off by certain worldly offerings—that they respond to such offerings in distinctive sensorimotor ways that exhibit a certain minimal kind of directedness and phenomenality. The important difference is that, in this revised version, responding in such ways to specific kinds of situations does not inherently "say" anything about how things stand with the world.

To reject that all mentality involves content requires abandoning even the idea that embrained vehicles of content exist. The fate of vehicles depends on the fate of content. If basic mentality isn't essentially contentful, then there are no vehicles of basic mentality. No vehicles reside anywhere in the brain, the alleged seat of the mind. To see why this follows, it helps to be reminded that the distinction between contents and their vehicles gets its life from an analogy with sentential, linguistic content. Neural vehicles are said to bear mental contents in essentially the same way that sentences bear linguistic contents. Hence, we are able to easily understand the important differences between vehicles and contents in this model. Drawing on this very example, Dretske (1995) reminds us that it makes no sense to say that the entities and events represented in a story (its contents) reside in a book. No one expects to find damsels in distress, brave knights, or feats of derring-do in books. But it makes perfect sense to think that sentences describing those events (the vehicles of those linguistically conveyed contents) can be found in specific locations in a book. By the same token, it is assumed that neural vehicles of mental content can, in principle, be located in specific places in brains, even though it would be a mistake to think of mental contents as located there.[7]

The situation looks quite different to anyone who denies that basic mentality involves content, as REC does. This is because doing so requires giving up thinking of the substrate of experiential responses as content-carrying vehicles. In chapter 4 we will show why REC is justified in rejecting the idea that basic cognition is a matter of responding to or consuming contents.

REC rejects all vestiges of the model upon which the distinction between mental contents and vehicles rests.

On the positive side, having made this important adjustment to Dretske's theory, we can retain something from it that is very close, if not identical, to the enactivist idea that the distinctive quality of experiencing boils down to specifiable ways of responding. Here it is worth quoting Dretske at length:

> Our mental states *not only* have a reference, an aboutness, an object (or purported object) that forms their topic; they represent *that object in one way rather than another*. When an object is represented, there is always an aspect under which it is represented. Even when there is no object, the aspect remains. The same is true of the objects we experience. The objects I see *look a certain way* to me—red, round, and stationary. The objects I touch *feel a certain way to me*—rough and cold. Experiences are of objects, yes, but one cannot experience an object without experiencing it under some aspect. (1995, p. 31, emphases added)

Although we agree with Dretske that there are different ways of experiencing the same thing, we identify these ways of experiencing with specific aspectual ways of responding, rather than with aspectual representations—with contents, as Dretske does.

Why on earth would anyone contemplate making such a foundational adjustment to Dretske's theory? We will argue in chapter 4 that defenders of CIC face an intractable problem, which we will call the Hard Problem of Content. This problem arises when they try to make their favored notion of informational content credible to explanatory naturalists. In a nutshell, the notion of informational content they require is too metaphysically extravagant to be accepted by hard-nosed naturalists.

A pure form of teleosemantics—one that avoids any troublesome commitment to the independent existence of informational content—is the next best hope of securing the fortunes of unrestricted CIC. But a pure teleosemantics faces problems in accounting for the properties needed to explain the required mental content. Hence, we aim to show that the most promising accounts of content—those on which the proponents of unrestricted CIC rely—fail. But we also show that this shouldn't trouble those working in cognitive science, since there is no real explanatory advantage in positing contentful mental states at the level of basic cognition in any case.

Rather than investing more intellectual effort in shoring up unrestricted CIC by attempting to fix the fundamental problems faced by existing theories of content, we recommend placing bets on and developing REC. Our aim is to discourage belief in and commitment to the idea that basic minds are content involving through a series of "can't have" and "don't need" arguments. Before turning to that task, it is instructive to highlight the ways in which REC differs from other less radical versions of enactivism.

2 Enactivisms Less Radical

He who does not see things in their depth should not call himself a radical.

—José Marti

Other Enactivisms

A truly radical enactivism differs in important respects from the more conspicuous and already well-established branches of enactivism—*Sensorimotor Enactivism* and *Autopoietic Enactivism*. While REC shares much with, and owes much, to its sister accounts, there are significant differences between some of its commitments and what is on offer in these frameworks. In this chapter we highlight these and identify what we take to be the most serious and fundamental challenge facing any bona fide content-free version of enactivism.

Sensorimotor Enactivism

Like its more radical relative, Sensorimotor Enactivism promotes the view that perception, action, and perceptual experience are inescapably connected (Hurley 1998; O'Regan and Noë 2001; Hurley and Noë 2003; Noë 2004, 2009). The position is known for slogans telling us that perceiving and perceptual experience "isn't something that happens in us, it is something we do" (Noë 2004, p. 216) and that such phenomena are "realized in the active life of the skilful animal" (ibid., p. 227).

These Sensorimotor Enactivist claims can be read as concerning essentially personal-level phenomena—phenomena to be found nowhere else than in—and certainly nowhere short of—concrete, extended, and interactive organismic engagements (Ward, forthcoming). Consequently, activity in neural substrates that helps to make perceiving and perceptual experience possible is necessary but not sufficient for the occurrence of these phenomena. In line with this, Sensorimotor Enactivists criticize views that seek to identify such phenomena with the production of inner images or mental representations. This is seen most clearly in their trademark rejection of the idea that a rich and detailed inner representation is formed whenever perceiving occurs.

Perceiving is, according to this approach, not an internal process aimed at the production of a percept inside the brain, but rather a process of interaction between organism and environment. Perceiving is navigating and acting in an environment, and it is possible without the staged generation of internal representational products. Internal processes that manipulate information to produce representations, it is proclaimed, are to be traded in for external actions and movements of the organism. Perceptual sensitivity is sensitivity to relations between changes in simulation and movements. Instead of internally representing visual scenes in their full detail, perceivers shift their gaze to whatever in the world prompts or calls for attention.

Despite advancing such daring claims, the most prominent version of Sensorimotor Enactivism remains significantly conservative. It embraces intellectualist ideas that are rejected by

REC. In Noë 2004 (a more or less official philosophical state-ment of Sensorimotor Enactivism), these commitments appear in two places. First, there is the claim that perceptual experience is grounded in the possession and the use of implicit, practical *knowledge*. Second, there is the claim that perceptual experience is inherently representationally contentful, and that accordingly experience necessarily presents things as being a certain way. Thus "all perception is intrinsically thoughtful" (p. 3).

It is useful for our demarcation efforts to briefly review these claims and their implications. Consider the first of these com-mitments. Sensorimotor Enactivism's definitive thesis is that perceiving and enjoying perceptual experiences is mediated and made possible by the possession and skillful deployment of spe-cialized practical knowledge of sensorimotor contingencies—the ways in which stimulation in a certain sense modality changes, contingent upon movements or actions of the organism.[1]

Knowledge of this special sort is meant to account for the expectations that perceivers have concerning how things will appear in the light of possible actions; it amounts to knowing how things will manifest themselves if the environment is per-ceptually explored in certain ways. It follows that, at some level, perceivers (or their brains) must have implicit mastery of rel-evant laws concerning sensorimotor contingencies.

This proposal runs into difficulties when attempts are made to coherently and non-vacuously articulate the precise nature of the knowledge in question—and especially how it can play the kind of mediating role it is assigned by this theory. In particular, it doesn't seem possible to tell a consistent story about how such knowledge is essentially practical yet nevertheless mediating.

This tension begins to make itself apparent if one attends to the sorts of description that sensorimotor enactivists typically give when explicating the nature of the so-called implicit, practical knowledge in question. Although they insist that perception and its experience is based on a kind of know how, they tend to fall into unguarded talk of perceivers' (or their brains') making assumptions, predictions, and judgments in ways that look decidedly as if the view is committed to the existence of propositional rather than essentially practical knowledge.[2] This makes it appear as if the sort of knowledge that putatively grounds sensorimotor understanding is, on this account, really a kind of knowing that. (See Hutto 2005; Rowlands 2007.) If that is so, it is hard to see how the sensorimotor knowledge in question is essentially a kind of practical knowledge—at least, in any interesting sense.[3] Even if such knowledge were entirely practical—even if achieving practical ends was its sole concern—the nature and form of the knowledge in question might be grounded in a set of semantically contentful sub-personal rules and representations. This is surely one option for making sense of Noë's claim that "sensorimotor understanding is in fact the ground of your possession of dispositions to respond to the presented object" (2004, p. 88).

It might be supposed that embracing this much representationalism by Sensorimotor Enactivism is a price well worth paying in order to make sense of how experience is grounded in mediating knowledge. This idea is especially attractive if one also thinks that only by appealing to such represented knowledge is it possible to make sense of what has to be added to sensory stimulation to yield full-blown perceptual experience—i.e., expectations about sensorimotor contingencies. After all, "the work of the enactive approach is done by perceivers' *expectations* of the sensory effects of movement" (Noë 2004, p. 119).

Talk of mediating knowledge is surely encouraged by the thought that the sum total of what we are experiencing at any time extends beyond what we are immediately presented with, a claim that all parties accept. Having an experience involves more than just having a series of discrete sensations—it involves having, *inter alia*, expectations about what is not directly experienced at a specific moment. For example, these expectations explain our feeling of the perceptual presence of whole objects, even when it is only their parts that are, strictly speaking, visible to us. The thought is that perception depends on anticipating possibilities for perceptually related actions even if such actions aren't taken.[4]

It is natural enough to want to make sense of the relevant expectations as a kind of mediating knowledge. Many philosophers will cash out the same idea by appealing to mental representations. Going representationalist is certainly one option. That Noë wishes to take it is suggested by his occasionally parading Sensorimotor Enactivism's intellectualism as a virtue. For example, he avers that perception and perceptual experience depend on the possession and use of practical knowledge, and that this is what distinguishes Sensorimotor Enactivism as a brand of cognitivism. This, apparently, allows him to deny the charge that he is a closet behaviorist. (See Noë 2004, p. 33.)

Fair enough. But if this really is the sort of account that Sensorimotor Enactivists are offering, then at best they are making only a very modest advance on standard intellectualist approaches—at best, they conservatively endorse only CEC and not REC. Thus, their proposal incurs the same costs that all other CIC approaches incur. Ultimately, anyone pursuing this sort of line must face up to the problems of providing a theory that would explain the source and the nature of perceptual, experiential content. In chapters 4–6 we will critically review the prospects of achieving this and question the motivations for trying.

Yet, in fact, Noë claims not to want to go this way. He is adamant that "sensorimotor knowledge is not propositional" (2004, p. 118); that it "is practical and not theoretical" (p. 88). For example, we are told:

It takes no thought or intellectual skill to know that to bring the item off to the left better into view, you must turn your head to the left . . . [or] when you hear a sound as being on the left you don't need to think about which way to turn your head in order to orientate toward the sound. . . . You do need to think about how to maneuver a couch to squeeze it through a small passage. But you do not need, in the same way, to think about how to maneuver your body to squeeze it through the doorway. Just perceiving the doorway as having certain spatial qualities is perceiving it as enabling, requiring, or permitting certain kinds of movements with respect to it. (p. 89)

Even so, Noë also holds that implicit practical knowing is something more than the exercise of behavioral dispositions. It is not clear how Noë can have his cake and eat it too on this issue. Whereas the endorsement of representationalism is coherent but costly, without that commitment there appears to be no way to specify in positive terms what kind of thing implicit practical knowledge is meant to be, given that it is not merely embodied in dispositions of organisms but is supposed to form the ground for such dispositions.

There are good reasons to be suspicious of the coherency of the idea of implicit, practical, but nevertheless mediating knowledge. Perhaps the most important reason is tied to the fact that "the mere passive storage of sensorimotor knowledge cannot plausibly determine the contents of a given experience" (Roberts 2010, p. 104). In places, Noë speaks as if possession of the relevant knowledge would suffice for experiencing. (See, e.g., pp. 2 and 89 of Noë 2004.) But to think that is unacceptable since experiencings are occurrent, not dispositional, events.

Merely possessing implicit (even if practical) knowledge of what to expect from certain sensorimotor explorations cannot be enough to explain how things actually appear to an experiencer on some occasion. If it were enough, one might passively possess such knowledge and fail to exercise it in any way. In such a case, possessing such knowledge could make no relevant difference to how things seem to a perceiver.

To correct for this, it might be held that if the imagined implicit practical knowledge is to do its required work it must be not only possessed but also actively exercised. Sensorimotor Enactivism does emphasize, after all, that the knowledge in question is not only possessed but also used. If this proposal is to work, the exercise of the knowledge cannot be a contingent requirement. It seems that the knowledge *must* be exercised in some way in order to yield experience.

Although accepting this necessity looks like the right move, it reveals what is problematic about the claim that we ought to understand perceptual experience as being mediated by knowledge in the first place. As we have just seen, if the idea the sensorimotor knowledge in question is essentially practical is to make sense, it can't be logically separated from use. As a result, the postulation of knowledge of an essentially practical variety is in tension with an important aspect of the official statement of the central thesis of Sensorimotor Enactivism. For it cannot be that perceptual experiences are grounded in mediating knowledge that is distinct from actual embodied tendencies of organisms that are exercised in some way.

If this analysis is correct, it reveals that what is on offer from Sensorimotor Enactivists is wholly unlike any standard cognitivist notion of knowledge. When cognitivists speak of a knowledge-based competence, they strongly distinguish the knowledge base itself from the activity of deploying it in performance. As Chomsky (1988) asserts (1988, p. 9), the main reason for adopting this line is because "the idea that knowledge is ability is . . . entirely untenable."

Alternatively, in line with the Developmental-Explanatory Thesis, an organism's current sensorimotor expectations might be accounted for by appealing to its history. And, in line with a strong reading of the Embodiment Thesis, it is not knowledge (embodied know-how) that gives perceptual experiences their intentionality and phenomenal character; rather; it is the concrete ways in which organisms actively engage with their environments. But in so engaging with their environments there is not a set of facts that organisms know, or need to know, at any level.

If talk of mediating knowledge is understood in this deflationary way, it is a red herring. And it surely follows that, despite its great emphasis on experience being grounded in knowledge, this would not make Sensorimotor Enactivism a properly intellectualist proposal that buys into CIC.

But Sensorimotor Enactivism is surely committed to intellectualism in another way: through its attachment to the idea that perceptual experience is inherently contentful. Noë avers that "perceptual experience presents things as being thus and such" and that "it has content" (2004, p. 189). This idea is connected with Noë's brand of enactivism in the following way: "[M]ere sensory stimulation becomes experience with world-presenting content thanks to the perceiver's possession [/exercise] of sensorimotor skills." (p. 183) Accordingly, "to see one must have visual impressions that one understands" (p. 6). Furthermore, Noë defends the view that such understanding is conceptual through and through against those who hold that perceptual content can be nonconceptual. He assumes that to perceive requires concepts of some kind, even if they are low-level or primitive.

In defending these ideas, Noë advances an essentially Kantian line, assuming that we bring concepts to bear on what is sensorily given, but he does so with an important twist: he adopts a quite unorthodox understanding of the nature of concepts. For him, concepts are abilities or "practical skills" (2004, p. 199). In this respect, Noë's position is complicated. He breaks rank with standard intellectualist accounts that regard concepts as discrete and meaningful thought contents—i.e., as representations. (See, e.g., Tye 2009, p. 39–40.)

Noë illustrates his idea that the exercise of conceptual understanding in the form of abilities gives rise to perceptual contents by means of an example. He claims that when we experience something as a cube "it is the concept cube that gives content to the experience" (2004, p. 207). Yet the concept of a cube is taken to be a concept based on nothing more than primitive sensorimotor skills. Here again, we are faced with a threat of collapse. For there is no possibility of understanding the kind of concepts that matter to having experiences, conceived of as practical skills, independently of how they are used in some way or other.

But having gone this far, why think experience is conceptual at all? We are inclined to think it isn't, because we find the notion of concept in play in Noë's account to be much too liberal and too individualistic. The bar for being a concept user is set very low if all that is required is having a skilled capacity for engaging with specific kinds of things in reliably expectant ways. For it is surely part of our attributional practice to count infants and animals as perceiving something on just these grounds, even though we would not necessarily credit them with a mastery of the concept of what they are perceiving or experiencing. The need to acknowledge such cases is an important reason for thinking that our most rudimentary forms of perceiving and perceptual experience are essentially nonconceptual.

In promoting REC, we reject not only the idea that basic mentality (which includes perceptual experience) is conceptually based but also the idea that it is inherently contentful. Noë, like many others, holds that mentality must be contentful because they take it that content is required in order to explain the intentional properties of perceptual experiences. After all, these are "directed toward" aspects of the environment and are "about the world" (Noë 2004, p. 189). And, as a bonus, if one thinks of such content as having full-fledged semantic properties, this warrants the idea that "in perception you 'entertain' a judgeable content" (p. 189).

Doubtless some experiences inspire conceiving, and even conceiving of things as being a certain way—i.e., of judging them to be thus and so.[5] But it hardly follows that this is a built-in feature of perceptual experiences. (In chapters 5 and 6 we will develop and motivate the idea that it is not a built-in feature.)

Autopoietic Enactivism

Autopoietic Enactivism is committed to the idea that mentality is something that emerges from the self-organizing and self-creating activities of living organisms. Carrying on in the footsteps of Varela, Thompson, and Rosch (1991), Thompson (2007) elaborates this variety of enactivism in greater detail. Thompson seeks to understand minds by placing them in the broader context of the conditions of living.

REC has strong affinities with Autopoietic Enactivism, especially because, unlike the Sensorimotor variety, Autopoietic Enactivism explicitly desires to make a complete break with cognitivism and representationalism (Thompson 2007, Di Paolo 2009). Autopoietic Enactivism advances a boldly anti-representationalist version of enactivism: it challenges, root and branch, the passive-cognitivist view of the mind-brain. It aims for nothing short of the eradication of the misleading dualisms that, despite challenges, continue to dominate analytic philosophy of mind and much of cognitive science.

Thompson sees the enactive approach as a way to put aside the mind-body problem once and for all. To adopt Thompson's approach is to give up on the traditional input-output processing model of the mind, which continues to pay homage, if only tacitly, to the idea of what is sensorially or informationally "given." It is to abandon the idea of informational content that is received or informs and, concomitantly, the idea that informational content is intellectually categorized, conceptualized, and schematized by higher forms of cognitive spontaneity. By reconceptualizing mentality in active, dynamic, and loopy terms, Thompson undermines traditional boundaries and dichotomies.

The boundaries thought to hold between mind and body and between mind and world are revealed to be, ultimately, of only heuristic value, having no genuine metaphysical import. Autopoietic Enactivism asks to trade in the modern, Cartesian picture of the mind as a sort of mechanism for a more Aristotelian vision of mentality that emphasizes its biological character and the special features it shares with all living systems.

On this view, instead of being directed by information captured in genes (in the case of life), or in inner representations (in the case of consciousness and cognition), the relevant structures become manifest only through a developmental process in which factors belonging to the organism and factors belonging to its environment play equally important roles.

REC agrees with Autopoietic Enactivism that a misleading notion of information has led to similar deep confusions about the nature of life and minds, and it concurs with the idea that it is plausible that mentality and life have basic organizational properties in common.

Still, there are some important differences—at least on the surface—between the two proposals. Recall that REC thoroughly abandons talk of contents and meanings at the level of basic mentality. In this respect it apparently goes further than Autopoietic Enactivism, for it rejects all remnants of the idea that organismic responses relevant to basic mentality are responses that create, carry, and consume meanings. By comparison, in discussing emotional responding, Thompson tells us that "sensory stimuli . . . induce the construction by nonlinear dynamics of an activity pattern in the form of large-scale spatial pattern of coherent oscillatory activity. This pattern is not a representation of the stimulus but an endogenously generated response triggered by the sensory perturbation, a response that *creates and carries the meaning* of the stimulus for the animal. This meaning reflects the individual organism's history, state of expectancy, and environmental context." (2007, p. 368, emphasis added) This way of putting things has encouraged other enactivists to make bolder claims. Colombetti underscores the "meaning-generating" role of the body when she speaks of the non-neural body as a "vehicle of meaning" (2010, pp. 146, 147) and asserts that "*meaning* is generated within the system for the system itself—that is, it is generated and at the same time consumed by the system" (p. 148).

Although Colombetti specifies that the meaning in question is always relational and co-determined by the organism and its environment, it is not clear how to make sense of the metaphors of production and consumption or how to understand what is consumed or produced. Taken at face value, they suggest additional, special processes that are somehow distinct from the way an organism responds to the worldly offerings in intentionally directed and perhaps emotionally charged ways. But if talk of meaning and vehicles of meaning doesn't imply distinct and additional processes, it isn't clear what work it does in these accounts.

Another difference is that advocates of Autopoietic Enactivism tend to operate with a quite liberal understanding of the nature of cognition. Thompson (2007, p. 125) proposes that "cognitive interactions are those in which sensory responses guide action and actions have consequences for subsequent sensory stimulation, subject to the constraint that the system maintains its viability. 'Sensory response' and 'action' are taken broadly to include, for example, a bacterium's ability to sense the concentration of sucrose in its immediate environment and to move itself accordingly."

Talk of "cognition," "interpretation," "sense-making," "understanding," and even "emoting" in describing the responses of simple living systems is misplaced and misleading. Proponents of Autopoietic Enactivism admit this to an extent. On this score, they give but quickly take away. Varela, Thompson, and Rosch (1991) note that they use the terms 'significance' and 'relevance' advisedly in speaking of simple creatures enactively bringing forth their worlds. Consequently, even though Varela et al. assume that some kind of interpretation takes place in such cases, they confess that "this interpretation is a far cry from the kinds of interpretation that depend on experience" (p. 156). We are inclined to take a harder line: This is no kind of interpretation. The simplest life forms are capable of an intentionally directed responding of a kind that when suitably augmented provides a necessary platform for cognition, interpretation, understanding, sense-making, and emoting; however, their activities do not, in and of themselves, qualify as these forms of mentality.

Still, there seems no reason to rule out the possibility that such activity constitutes a basic kind of intentional directedness—an intentional directedness of a sort that is shared with more sophisticated forms of life that possess more elaborate minds. The ultimate task is to explain how basic minds make the development of contentful forms of cognition possible when the right supports, such as shared social practices, are in place.

The more modest claim, which we endorse, is that basic interest-driven ways of responding provide the right platform for understanding how mentality can be intentionally directed yet also wholly embodied and enactive. Certain organisms are not only set up so that they are intentionally directed at situations that can bear on their interests; in some cases, their ways of responding are also phenomenally charged. This is possible despite the fact that such responding lacks content and is wholly non-representational.

The Information-Processing Challenge

Having clarified how REC differs from Sensorimotor Enactivism and Autopoietic Enactivism in particular respects, we are now in a position to deal with the greatest threat to REC—the most persuasive reason for rejecting it in favor of some variant of CIC. REC faces the charge that a wholesale rejection of the idea that basic minds are contentful commits the cardinal sin of failing to recognize that mentality is essentially "grounded in processes of information extraction, transformation and use" (Clark 2008b, p. 19).

The Information-Processing Challenge appears to present a formidable problem for REC. But it takes for granted that the standard computational and information-processing explanatory strategies of cognitivism are in perfectly good order under standard renderings. To take this for granted is to accept, without argument, what Thompson identifies as the received view in cognitive science—a view that is committed to the idea that "in order to explain cognitive abilities we need to appeal to information-bearing states inside the system. Such states, by virtue of the semantic information they carry about the world, qualify as representations" (2007, p. 52, emphasis added).

The conservative wing of cognitive science insists that intelligence depends on information processing. As the quotation from Clark presented above reminds us, information is thought to be the basic currency of cognition. Information is received, stored, manipulated, and transformed by intelligent systems. It is the necessary fuel for truly cognitive engines.

In short, the complaint is that any radical, content-free, and anti-representational version of enactivism, including REC, fails to appreciate the fundamental role of content-using information processes in defining mental activity, and indeed in making it possible. We call this the Information-Processing Challenge. We answer the challenge in chapter 4, where we expose that explanatory naturalists can't have informational content of the sort needed to make this objection work.

The conclusion that informational content is not naturalistically respectable may come as something of a shock. If accepted it can lead to skepticism about the tenability of classic representational and computational explanatory strategies in cognitive science. We soften the blow in chapter 3, preparing the reader for the bitter pill by first providing reasons for thinking that content-based accounts are neither needed nor best placed to explain a wide range of important mental phenomena anyway. In other words, we make a start on dealing with a familiar scope objection to REC.

3   The Reach of REC

Everyone imposes his own system as far as his army can reach.
—Joseph Stalin

Reckoning with REC

An obvious line of argument against REC draws on observations about the proper order and requirements of bona fide cognitive explanations—on presumed explanatory needs. Fodor (2008b) hopes to dispatch REC by observing that positing contentful, representationally based thinking is the minimum requirement for explaining any and all activity that deserves the accolade "intelligent responding"—an observation predicated on the assumption that we can draw a principled bright line between what is properly cognitive and what is not. Accordingly, Fodor insists that we have no choice but to accept that "the ability to think the kind of thoughts that have truth-values is, in the nature of the case, prior to the ability to plan a course of action. The reason is perfectly transparent: Acting on plans (as opposed to, say, merely behaving reflexively or just thrashing about) requires being able to think about the world." (ibid., p. 13) In a nutshell, this is Fodor's master argument for thinking that prag-matist REC-style approaches to the mind *must* be false: to think the kinds of thoughts that have truth-values is to think thoughts with representational content and, presumably, to make plans requires manipulating these representations (and their components) computationally.[1] In short, if *all* bona fide intelligent action involves planning, and all bona fide planning involves computing and representation, then this is bad news from the front line for REC rebels.

Without a doubt, some problems (indeed, perhaps whole classes of problems) are best addressed through advanced careful planning—planning of the sort that requires the rule-governed manipulation of truth-evaluable representations. Sometimes it is not only advisable but utterly necessary to stand back and assess a situation in a relatively detached manner, drawing explicitly on general background propositional knowledge of situations of a similar type and using that knowledge to decide—say, by means of deduction and inference—what would be the correct or the most effective approach. This can be done before initiating any action or receiving any live feedback from the environment, and it is the preferred strategy for dealing with certain situations, such as defusing bombs, in which a trial-and-error approach is not advisable. Making use of remote representations also works well for some mundane tasks—for example, figuring out the best route from the train station to one's hotel in a foreign city from the comfort of one's office, long before boarding a plane. Such intelligent planning can be done at a remove, and reliably, if it is possible to exploit and manipulate symbolic representations of the target domain on the assumption that one has the requisite background knowledge and can bring that knowledge to bear. This works if the domain itself is stable over time, since stability will ensure that any stored representations remain current and accurate. By using representations of a well-behaved domain's features and properties, and having a means of knowing determinately what to expect if the domain changes under specific modifications and permutations, a problem solver can plan how to act within the domain without ever having to (or ever having had to) interact with it in a first-hand manner. This is, of course, the ideal end state of high theoretical science.

As natural language users, we humans are representation mongers of this sort and thus regularly adopt this basic strategy to solve problems. Our cultural heritage provides us with a store of represented knowledge—in many formats—that enables us to do so, successfully, under the sorts of conditions just mentioned. But it hardly follows that this type of cognitive engagement is the basis of, is required for, or is suitable for all sorts of tasks, always and everywhere. Echoing Ryle (1949), Noë notes that "the real problem with the intellectualist picture is that it takes rational deliberation to be *the most basic kind of cognitive operation*" (2009, p. 99, emphasis added).

Intellectualism of this unqualified kind—of the sort that assumes the existence of strongly detached symbolic representations of specific target domains across the board—has fallen on hard times. Today it finds only a few unflagging adherents in cognitive science. Indeed, if anything has promoted the fortunes of REC it has been the dismal failure of the standard "rules and representation" approach when it comes to dealing with the most basic forms of intelligent activity. This is the headline-grabbing lesson of recent efforts in robotics and artificial intelligence, which have provided what appear to be a series of existence proofs against the idea that basic cognition is CIC.

Pioneering work by Brooks (1991a,b) and Beer (1996) reveals that intellectualism is a bad starting point when thinking about how to build robots that actually work. Important lessons have been learned by paying attention to the architectonic requirements of robots that are able to complete quite basic tasks, such as navigating rooms while avoiding objects or recognizing simple geometrical forms and shapes. Inverting standard intellectualist thinking, Brooks famously rejected the Sense-Model-Plan-Act approach, and built robots that dynamically and frequently sample features of their local environments in order to directly guide their responses. They do so without going through the extra steps of generating and working with descriptions of those environments.

Brooks' first-generation behavior-based robots, and those that followed, succeed precisely because their behaviors are directly guided by continuous, temporally extended interactions with aspects of their environments, rather than being based on represented internal knowledge about those domains (knowledge that would presumably be stored somewhere in the robots' innards).

The overarching principle behind Brooks' so-called subsumption architectures is that sensing is connected with appropriate responding in a representationally unmediated way, even if indefinitely many interacting subsystems are causally involved in such responding. Crucially, the great success of these artificial agents demonstrates that it is possible for a being to act intelligently without creating and relying on internal representation and models. Very much in line with theoretical worries raised by the frame problem, it may even be that, when it comes to basic cognition, this is the only real possibility.

Nature provides additional support for the same conclusion. Webb's (1994, 1996) work on cricket phonotaxis offers a vivid example of a model of how successful navigation takes place in the wild, apparently without the need for representations or their manipulation. Female crickets locate and move toward mates by attending to the acoustic signals of male songs, frequently adjusting the path of their approach accordingly. The male songs they attune to have a species-specific characteristic tone and rhythm—one that uniquely matches the particular makeup of the female's auditory system, which is capable of responding only to these species-specific signals. Females' orienting and moving toward singing males is a direct result of the physical path of the male's acoustic signals in the sensory system of the female. In other words, the capacity of these animals to adjust their behavior when successfully locating mates requires them to engage in a continuous interactive process of engagement with the environment. In doing so, they exploit special features of their bodies (including the unique design of their auditory mechanism) as well as special features of the environment (the characteristic acoustic pattern of the male songs). In this case a beautiful cooperation arises because of the way the cricket's body and features of the wider environment enable successful navigational activity—activity that involves nothing more than a series of dynamic and regular embodied interactions.

How insects and behavior-based robots make their way in the world is well known and has been much discussed. (For excellent summaries, see Clark 2001, Wheeler 2005, and Shapiro 2011.) For the purposes of this chapter it suffices to note that these observations, when bolstered by the articulation of a supporting theoretical framework provided by dynamical systems theory, offer a serious and well-known challenge to the CIC assumptions of intellectualist cognitive science. (For further discussion, see Beer 1998, 2000; Thompson 2007; Garzón 2008; Chemero 2009.)

In sum, what the foregoing reflections teach us is that there are cases in which bodily and environmental factors play ineliminable and non-trivial parts in making certain types of cognition possible. One familiar intellectualist response to these sorts of examples is to try to cast these wider contributions as playing no more than causal supporting roles that, even if necessary to enable cognition, don't constitute it or form part of it. For reasons that should be obvious from the foregoing discussion, it is not clear how one might motivate this interpretation in a non-question-begging manner and make it convincing with respect to the sorts of cases just described.

In rejecting CIC in this domain, REC takes at face value what attending to the architectonic details of how these agents work suggests: that the specified bodily and environmental factors are equal partners in constituting the embodied, enactive intelligence and cognition of these artificial and natural agents. Accordingly, although for certain practical purposes and interventions it may be necessary to carve off and focus on specific causally contributing factors in isolation, the cognitive activity itself cannot be seen as other than "a cyclical and dynamic process, with no nonarbitrary start, finish, or discrete steps" (Hurley 2008, p. 12; see also Garzón 2008, p. 388). Or, put otherwise, when it comes to understanding cognitive acts "the agent and the environment are non-linearly coupled, they, together constitute a nondecomposable system" (Chemero 2009, p. 386).

In promoting this framework, REC highlights the "real danger" that "the explanatory utility of representation talk may evaporate altogether" (Wheeler 2005, p. 200). As Shapiro (2011) notes, the interesting question is whether an anti-representationalist paradigm has real prospects of replacing intellectualist cognitive science altogether. And Shapiro is right to suppose that the two main "sources of support for Replacement come from (i) work that treats cognition as emerging from a dynamical system and (ii) studies of autonomous robots" (p. 115). Though anti-representationalism is potentially powerful, just how far it might take us remains to be seen. To make a convincing case for our far-reaching revolutionary ambitions, as proponents of REC we must take the next step and "argue that *much or most cognition* can be built on the same principles that underlie the robot's intelligence" (ibid., p. 116, emphasis added).

Rather than deny the very possibility of non-representational cognition, intellectualists might take heart from this challenge and agree to split the difference, allowing that very basic forms of cognition—that is, cognition of the sort exemplified by robot and insect intelligence—might be suitable for REC treatment, but not other forms of cognition. This is to adopt a kind of containment strategy—a kind of theoretical kettling or corralling.

Some intellectualists might be tempted to concede that supporters of REC have a point, up to a point. Such intellectualists allow that "representations are not necessary for coordinated responses to an environment with which one is dynamically engaged" (Shapiro 2011, p. 153). But this concession would be made in the secure knowledge that it "would support only the conclusion that agents do not require representations for certain kinds of activities. However, a stronger conclusion, for instance that cognition never requires representational states, does not follow." (ibid., p. 153)

REC approaches dealing with most cases of bona fide cognition would be, accordingly, of limited value, on the assumption that they won't scale up. Call this the Scope Objection. It allows one to accept certain anti-representationalist lessons learned from the lab and nature while safe in the knowledge that even if representations aren't needed to explain the most basic forms of cognition this doesn't pose an interesting threat to intellectualism. No such threat ensues, because the sorts of cases in question "represent too thin a slice of the full cognitive spectrum" (ibid., p. 156). This assessment fits snugly with the oft-cited claim that some behavior is too off-line and representation hungry to be explained without appeal to the manipulation of symbolic representations. In particular, non-representational cognition, which might suffice for simple robots and animals, isn't capable of explaining properly world-engaging, human forms of cognition. But should that assessment prove mistaken—that is, should REC approaches make substantial inroads into explaining important forms of human cognition—then the boot might just be on the other foot, for it might turn out that representationally hungry tasks make up only a very small portion of mental activity. Representationally based cognition might be just the tip of the cognitive iceberg.

A Helping Hand

It cannot be denied that a great deal of human manual activity is connected with sophisticated forms of cognition. Milner and Goodale's (1995) famous neuropsychological studies reveal that humans can perform remarkably demanding manual acts—acts requiring the exercise of very fine-grained motor capacities, such as posting letters through slots with changing orientations—with precision even when they lack the capacity to explicitly report upon or describe the visual scenes they are dealing with. Nor, with only rare exceptions, is it credible that humans normally learn how to use their hands in these sorts of ways by means of explicit, contentfully mediated instruction, the rules for which only later becoming submerged and tacit. It is not as if children are taught by their caregivers through explicit description how to grasp or reach for items. A far more plausible hypothesis is that we become handy through a prolonged history of interactive encounters—through practice and habit. An individual's manual know-how and skills are best explained entirely by appealing to a history of previous engagements and not by the acquisition of some set of internally stored mental rules and representations. This looks, essentially, to be as clear a case as any of a process of "laying down a path in walking" or, in this case, "handling."

If it should turn out that much human manual activity is best explained without appeal to the manipulation of rules or representations, defenders of REC will have made significant progress in addressing the Scope Objection. REC approaches will have shown the capacity to advance well beyond dealing with the antics of behavior-based robots and insects, having moved deep into the heart of distinctively human cognition.

Are there grounds for thinking that manual activity is best explained in a CIC-free way? Tallis' philosophically astute and empirically informed examination of the hand provides an excellent starting point for addressing this question. Tallis claims that "the hand [is] . . . an organ of cognition" and is so "in its own right" (2003, pp. 28, 31). This is not to say that the hand works in isolation from the brain; indeed, Tallis characterizes the hand as the "brain's most versatile and intelligent lieutenant" (p. 22). Of course, this way of putting things suggests that the hand is, when all goes well, in some way nothing but a faithful subordinate—one that works under top-down instruction and guidance. This underestimates the bi-directional interplay between manual and brain activity—interplay of the sort that explains why the distinctive manual dexterity of *Homo sapiens,* which sets us apart even from other primates who also have remarkable abilities in this regard, may have been one of the "main drivers" of the growth of the human brain (ibid., p. 22).

These ideas can be taken much further if one fully rejects what Tallis calls the "standard ploy" invoked by movement physiologists: that "'calculations' that the brain (or part of it) 'does' . . . permit customisation of the [motor] programs to the singularities of the individual action" (p. 65, emphases added)

Invoking the "standard ploy" amounts to assuming the existence of representational contents that specify and fill out hypothesized motor plans and motor programs that specify and supply instructive orders from the brain. Accordingly, this—and nothing else—lends intelligence to and directs manual activity. For example, on this view motor plans, intentions, and programs are understood as "propositional attitudes with contents of the form 'let [my] effector E perform motor act M with respect to goal-object G'" (Goldman 2009, p. 238).[2]

The trouble is that, even if we imagine that such representational contents exist, it is difficult to see how they could do the required work. They would have a chance of specifying what is to be done, and how it is to be done, only if they could go beyond issuing very general and abstract instructions of the sort that Goldman gestures at.

Only very fine-grained instructions would be capable of directing or controlling specific acts of manual activity successfully. This raises a number of questions. How do brains decide what general kind of motor act is the appropriate sort of motor act to use in any given situation? This, alone, is no simple thing, in view of the variety of possible manual acts.[3]

Even if we put that concern aside, proponents of the view that brains can initiate and control manual acts by traditional intellectualist means are left with the problem of explaining how and on what basis the brain decides how to execute any particular act. A major problem for the strict instructionalism of traditional intellectualism—in which all acting is preceded by a plan—is that the requirements for successfully performing any particular motor act are tied to a unique and changing context. For example, even if everything else remains static, the speed, the angle of approach, and the grip aperture have to be altered appropriately at successive stages as one does something as simple as picking up a coffee cup. In a nutshell:

[A] particular challenge . . . has been to explain how cognition and perception processes regulate complex multi-articular actions in dynamic environments. The problem seeks to ascertain how the many degrees of freedom of the human motor system (roughly speaking the many component parts such as muscles, limb segments, and joints) can be regulated by an internally represented algorithm . . . and how the motor plan copes with the on-going interaction between the motor system and energy fluxes surrounding the system, e.g., frictional forces and gravitational forces. . . . Not even the attempt to distinguish between the motor plan and the motor program has alleviated the problem in the literature. (Araújo and Davids 2011, p. 12; see also Summers and Anson 2009)

Successful manual activity requires customization on the fly. Hence, it is deeply implausible that the brain can identify what is required to successfully complete a certain type of activity by simply issuing general instructions to be carried out by ordering the implementation of pre-programmed routines. The implausibility of this suggestion is underscored by the fact that "most of the things we do are unique even though they may have stereotyped components" (Tallis 2003, p. 67).

Not surprisingly, human manual activity—despite its unique complexities—seems to depend on interactions among the brain, the body, and the environment—interactions that involve essentially the same kinds of dynamic interactive feedback and temporally extended engagements needed to explain the intelligent antics of behavior-based robots and insects.

In rejecting the standard ploy in favor of an REC-based approach, it is important to be aware that the cases of manual activity of interest are not—if we go by the strict concept of action—actions. If we operate with a strict concept of action, there is a constitutive connection between actions and intentional states. Accordingly, actions are conceived of as requiring the existence of propositional attitudes of some sort. But all that follows from this, as Rowlands observes, is that "most of what we do does not count as action" (2006, p. 97).

Respecting the stipulated criterion for what is required for action, many philosophers acknowledge the existence of non-intentional doings, motivated activities, and/or deeds. For example, Velleman (2000, p. 4) recognizes the need to "define a category of ungoverned activities, distinct from mere happenings, on the one hand, and from autonomous actions, on the other. This category contains the things one does rather than merely undergoes, but that one somehow fails to regulate in the manner that separates autonomous human action from merely motivated activity."

On the face of it, most animal doings take the form of sophisticated forms of highly coordinated, motivated activity that falls short of action if acting requires the forming of explicit (though perhaps non-conscious or even sub-personal) intentions and deliberate planning. Far from being mere "thrashings about" or "reflexive behaviors," such unplanned engagements appear to be quite skillful, and sometimes even expert, dealings with the world. If REC has the right resources for explaining the wide class of such doings, then it has the potential to explain quite a lot of what matters to us when it comes to understanding mind and cognition.

The Non-Standard Ploy: CIC Rescued?

Despite all that has been said in favor of REC, many will balk at going so far. There are weaker and much more conservative and conciliatory ways of taking on board what is best in embodied and enactive ideas without abandoning CIC in this domain in a wholesale way. Recall that several authors have proposed extended bodily states and processes might—at least on occasion—serve as vehicles carrying representational or informational content. As such, they can play special computational roles in enabling some forms of cognition (Clark 2008a). These conservative proposals about enactive and embodied cognition are perfectly compatible with CIC—that is, with asserting that "the mind is essentially a thinking or representing thing" (Clark 2008b, p. 149).

As we discussed in chapter 1, those who endorse only CEC and not REC may see the new developments in cognitive science not as posing a threat to the existing intellectualist paradigm but as supplying new tools with considerable potential to augment rather than undermine CIC. According to those who adopt this view, the cases of basic cognition described in the first section of this chapter are cases of bona fide cognition. But they imply CIC, although the most promising CIC proposal about such cases comes in the form of CEC. REC is false across the board.

CEC-style thinking is the most plausible way to save the contentful baby from the embodied bathwater. Its principle resource is to posit the existence of action-oriented representations. According to Wheeler, who has done more than most to promote this view, an action-oriented representation is one that is

(i) action-specific (tailored to a particular behavior and designed to represent the world in terms of specifications for possible actions);
(ii) egocentric (features bearer-relative content as epitomized by spatial maps in an egocentric co-ordinate system);
(iii) intrinsically context-dependent (the explicit representation of context is eschewed in favor of situated special-purpose adaptive couplings that implicitly define the context of activity in their basic operating principles). (2008, pp. 371–372; see also Wheeler 2005, p. 199)

Believing in action-oriented representations is consistent with accepting the Neural Assumption—an assumption that pays homage to the intuition that neural states and processes have a special cognitive status. Those attracted to this assumption believe it should be respected because, even though non-neural factors can qualify as representational vehicles, in most cases they do not. Still, the great majority of cognitive explanations only ever involve representations that are wholly brain-bound. This is so even in cases in which it is necessary to make appeal to extra-neural but non-representational causal factors in order to explain the specific way some particular intelligent activity unfolds. By accepting this last caveat, defenders of CEC allow that the full explanation of a bout of intelligent behavior need not be strongly instructional in the way demanded by the standard ploy.

Wheeler (2005) highlights the central features of CEC-style thinking, illustrating the role that action-oriented representations are hypothesized to play in the architecture of a simple behavior-based robot created by Francheschini, Pichon, and Blanes (1992):

The robot has a primary visual system made up of a layer of elementary motion detectors (EMDs). Since these components are sensitive only to movement, the primary visual system is blind at rest. What happens, however, is that the EMD layer *uses* relative motion *information*, generated by the robot's own bodily motion during the previous movement in the sequence to build a temporary *snap map* of the detected obstacles, constructed using an egocentric coordinate system. Then, in an equally temporary *motor map, information* concerning the angular bearing of those detected obstacles is *fused with information* concerning the angular bearing of the light source (supplied by a supplementary visual system) and a directional heading for the next movement is generated. (Wheeler 2005, p. 196, first, second, fifth and sixth emphases added)

Wheeler considers and dismisses a number of possible minimal criteria for being an action-oriented representation, some of which make appeal to selectionist strategies and decoupleability. After careful review, he settles on the idea that what is necessary and sufficient to distinguish behavior-based systems that operate with action-oriented representations is that such systems exhibit arbitrariness and homuncularity. A system exhibits arbitrariness just when the equivalence class of different inner elements is fixed "by their capacity, when organized and exploited in the right ways, to carry specific items of information or bodies of information about the world" (Wheeler 2005, p. 218). A system is homuncular when (a) it can be compartmentalized into a set of hierarchically organized communicating modules and (b) each of those modules performs a well-defined sub-task that contributes toward the collective achievement of the overall adaptive solution.

For Wheeler, the linchpin holding this account of action-oriented representations together is that some cognitive systems are information-processing systems. Thus,

The connection between our two architectural features becomes clear once one learns that, in a homuncular analysis, the *communicating sub-systems* are conceptualized as *trafficking in the information that the inner vehicles carry*. So certain subsystems are interpreted as producing information that is then consumed downstream by other subsystems. (Wheeler 2005, p. 218, emphases added)

We can legitimately describe a cognitive system as employing action-oriented representations just in case it is a genuine source of adaptive richness and flexibility and it turns out that its subsystems use "information-bearing elements to stand in for worldly states of affairs in their communicative dealings" (Wheeler 2005, p. 219). Satisfaction of the above conditions is all that is required for the existence of weak or minimal representations. In the end, all of the weight in this account is placed on the idea that it suffices for minimal representations to be present in a system if it manipulates and makes use of informational content in well-defined ways.

This minimal notion of representation is, no doubt, attractive to cognitive scientists. For anyone in the field, it is utterly "textbook" to be told that information is a kind of basic commodity—the raw material of cognition. After all, "minds are basically processors of information; cognitive devices [for] receiving, storing, retrieving, modifying and transmitting information of various kinds" (Branquinho 2001, pp. xii–xiii). There is great latitude for thinking about the processes that make this possible.

Mental representations might come in a wide variety of forms; there being no commitment in the claim itself to a specific kind of representation or to a particular sort of representational vehicle. . . . Mental representations might be thought of as images, schemas, symbols, models, icons, sentences, maps and so on. (p. xiv).

Accordingly, representations or representational vehicles "are items in the mind or brain of a given system that in some sense 'mirror', or are mapped onto, other items or sets of items . . . in the world" (p. xiv). Something is a vehicle iff it bears content. Something is a representation iff it possesses content. Content is crucial. Thus,

The whole thrust of cognitive science is that there are sub-personal contents and sub-personal operations that are truly cognitive in the sense that these operations can be properly *explained only in terms of these contents*. (Seager 1999, p. 27, emphasis added)

Dietrich and Markman define representations as "any internal state that mediates or plays a mediating role between a system's inputs and outputs *in virtue of that state's semantic content*" and define semantic content "*in terms of information* causally responsible for the state, and in terms of the use to which that information is put" (2003, p. 97, emphases added). In sum, believing in action-oriented representations minimally requires acceptance of "the general idea of inner states that bear contents" (Clark 2002, p. 386). In view of this, it might be thought that accepting that at least some cognitive systems employ action-oriented representations is a no-brainer. Certainly, it seems that this must be true of human manual activity of the sort described in the preceding section—activity of the sort that, if our argument goes through, would enable fans of REC to answer the Scope Objection. After all, even in cases in which that sort of activity isn't supported by focused, conscious perception, "the motor activity of the hand—reaching, gripping, and manipulation—cannot function in the absence of what is usually called 'sensory information'" (Tallis 2003, p. 27). Indeed, "the information the hand needs to support its manipulative function is most clearly evident in the first stage . . . in reaching out prior to grasping, shaping, etc. Here the hand is under primarily visual control: the target is located, the relationship to the body determined, the motion initiated to home in on the target—these are all regulated [or, better, assisted] by sight, which measures what needs to be done and the progress of the doing" (p. 27). With this in mind, it looks like manual activity is surely dependent on information-processing activity of the sort that would qualify as involving action-oriented representations—hence it is the sort of activity better suited to CEC than to REC. If so, any ground gained by supporters of REC in the preceding sections would be lost.

4   The Hard Problem of Content

[T]here is one kind of "information" appealed to in biology, Shannon's kind, that is unproblematic and does not require much philosophical attention. . . . This kind of information exists whenever there is ordinary contingency and correlation.

—Peter Godfrey Smith

Three in One Blow

It is good policy to kill two birds with one stone, whenever possible. This chapter seeks even greater economy. It has three birds in its sights:

(1) It aims to defang the informational-processing challenge mentioned at the end of chapter 2. That challenge threatens to promote the fortunes of some variant of unrestricted CIC over REC.

(2) It aims to show that proponents of CIC currently lack any naturalistically credible account of content upon which to ground their theorizing about basic minds. (If that is so, they have yet to secure their theoretical starting blocks.)

(3) It aims to show that, once the dust has settled, the leftovers from the failed CIC accounts provide the right basis for putting a REC account of basic mentality on a stable, positive footing.

All these ends are achieved by means of arguments designed to show, pivotally, that we don't need and can't have a CIC account of basic mentality—one which assumes that cognition essentially involves the acquisition and manipulation of informational contents.

Content—What Is It Good For?

Despite some obvious attractions, the action-oriented representation story and the support it lends to CIC via CEC over REC aren't beyond question. Indeed, anyone who favors unrestricted CIC, whether in traditional versions or under the auspices of CEC, must face up to the Hard Problem of Content—and we suggest that REC is a small price to pay for avoidance of that problem.

Before turning to that issue, it is worth highlighting an immediate concern about CEC and its reliance on action-oriented representations. Appeal to action-oriented representations seems to secure a future for new-style representationalism—apparently winning a critical metaphysical battle—but arguably at the cost of losing a wider explanatory war. For, on the assumption that action-oriented representations need not be decoupled in order to qualify as representations, their CEC defenders face the charge that "talk of representations in coupled systems may be too cheap, or too arbitrary, and thus adds little or nothing to an explanation of how these systems work" (Shapiro 2011, p. 147).[1] Chemero (2009) voices precisely this worry:

[T]he representational description of the system does not add much to our understanding of the system. . . . [Thus,] despite the fact that one can cook up a representational story once one has the dynamical explanation, the representational gloss does not predict anything about the system's behaviour that could not be predicted by dynamical explanation alone. (2009, p. 77)

This issue, initially cast as a purely explanatory concern, cannot be kept wholly free of metaphysical considerations. Focusing on an example from the game of cricket, Chemero observes that "in terms of the physics of the situation, the ball, the outfielder, and the intervening medium are just one connected thing. In effective tracking, that is, the outfielder, the ball, and the light reflected from the ball form a single coupled system. No explanatory purchase is gained by invoking representation here: in effective tracking, any internal parts of the agent that one might call mental representations are causally coupled with their targets." (ibid., p. 114)

The difficulty of establishing that hypothesized action-oriented representations make a real explanatory contribution is brought out by the fact that there doesn't appear to be any clear-cut way to decide which systems satisfy the relevant conditions for being minimally representational systems. For example, even today there are diverging opinions as to whether or not James Watt's much-discussed centrifugal governor—a device originally designed to ensure a constant operating speed in rotative steam engines—qualifies as a representational device (Van Gelder 1995). This is so despite the fact that those who take opposite views as to whether the governor uses representations are fully agreed about the characteristics of its internal design, which is quite elegant and simple. The Watt governor is designed so that the positions of its spindle arms interact with and modify the state of a valve that controls the engine's speed. When the arm is high, the valve slows the engine. When the arm is low, the valve increases the engine's speed.

In line with CEC criteria for action-oriented representations laid out in the preceding chapter, Chemero concludes that

It is possible to view the governor's arms as [noncomputational] representations. . . . It is the function of particular arm angles to change the state of the valve (the representation consumer) and so adapt it to the need to speed up or slow down. The governor was so designed . . . to play that role. . . . It is both a *map* and a *controller. It is an action oriented representation*, standing for the current need to increase or decrease speed.[2] (2009, p. 71, emphases added)

Shapiro dissents. After a careful review of this issue, he concludes that "Watt's design of the centrifugal governor *requires that* the angle of the flyball arms carry information about the flywheel speed in order to regulate the speed. Still, the function of the flyball arms is not to carry information, but rather to play a role in regulating the speed of the flywheel." (2011, p. 147) Shapiro's point is that in order for the governor to carry out its control function, the spindle arms must covary with the relevant changes in engine speed. That they carry information in this sense is an unavoidable, collateral feature of their design that enables them to perform their regulatory work. Apparently, this is not sufficient to qualify as being a true information processor in the relevant sense—hence the governor is misdescribed as making use of action-oriented representations.

Shapiro goes on to contrast the governor with other kinds of information-using devices. "Some devices," he holds, "surely do include components that have the function to carry information. The thermostat . . . is such a device. Thermostats contain a bimetal strip because the behavior of this strip carries information about [i.e. covaries with] temperature, and the room." (2011, p. 148)

The important difference for Shapiro is that, although the governor's arms carry information about the flywheel arms, the governor doesn't use that information to perform its control tasks. This is meant to mark the subtle but critical difference between merely complex systems and properly cognitive complex systems. Apparently, thermostatic systems are designed to use information about the temperature *as such* in carrying out their work.

One might be forgiven for failing to see the dramatic difference between the operation of thermostats and that of Watt governors. A thermostat regulates the system's temperature, maintaining it at a desired point. Its mechanisms exploit the properties of the bimetallic strip that—when all is well—responds in reliable ways to temperature changes, bending one way if heated and the opposite way if cooled. The important difference between the two types of systems is not that a thermostat involves more mechanisms or steps than a Watt governor. Rather, it is that the bimetallic strips in thermostats have the systemic function of indicating specific desired temperatures to other subsystems that use those indications to regulate their behavior. It is because they function in this special way that devices of this general type are representational—they exploit pre-existing indication relations, giving them the function to indicate how things stand externally and use those indications in particular ways.[3] According to Dretske, if such devices were naturally occurring they would "have a content, something *they say or mean*, that does not depend on the existence of our purposes and intentions. . . . [They would] have original intentionality, something they represent, say, or mean, that they do not get from us."[4] (1995, p. 8, emphasis added)

To qualify as representational, an inner state must play a special kind of role in a larger cognitive economy. Crudely, it must, so to speak, have the function of *saying or indicating* that things stand *thus and so*, and to be consumed by other systems because it says or indicates in that way. Moreover, even if it is assumed that an internal state or structure has such a function, it still has to meet Ramsey's (2007) standard to qualify as representational. Passing that test, or meeting the "job description challenge," requires "explaining how a physical state actually fulfills the role of representing in physical or computational process—accounting for the way something actually *serves* as a representation in a cognitive system" (2007, p. xv). As Ramsey makes clear, providing an account of content would answer that challenge only partly, for it asks how a physical structure comes to function as a representation, not merely how something that is already presumed to function as a representation acquires its content.

In the cases under examination, these worries are two sides of the same coin. It is plausible that many of the states (or ensembles of states) of systems that enable basic cognition are (1) merely reliably caused by (or nomically depend upon) the occurrence of certain external features, are (2) disposed to produce certain effects (under specific conditions), and (3) have been selected because of their propensities for properties 1 and 2. States or structures that only have properties 1–3 do not automatically qualify as truly contentful, thus representational. Having such properties does not entail having the proper function of saying that "things stand thus and so." Rather, they—like the mechanisms of the Watt governor—may only have the proper function to guide a system's responses with respect to specific kinds of worldly offerings. Even if such states serve to mediate responses, and even if they do so in highly complex ways, they can still fail to serve truly representational functions.

Exactly what else is required for being a representation-using system? Wheeler (2005) speaks of the need for communicative transactions between homuncular subsystems. On this view, trading in informational content is the basis of true cognition. Nonetheless, Wheeler acknowledges that this does not imply that the sub-systems "in any literal sense understand that information" (p. 218).

Fair enough. But even if the putative subsystems literally lack understanding of what they are dealing with, if this account is to have teeth those subsystems must nevertheless be literally trafficking in informational contents. They must be using and fusing these, even if they don't understand what such contents say. But talk of using and fusing contents, although quite common, cannot be taken literally either.

Theorists use a range of metaphors to describe what is done with information (and different kinds of information) in the fueling of cognitive activity. Information is said to be extracted, retrieved, picked up, fused, bounded up, integrated, brought together, stored, used for later processing, and so on and so forth. How seriously should we take this talk?

The (Literal) Truth about Information

What would information have to be if it were literally processed in the kinds of ways required by defenders of CIC? On the rare occasions when this is specified, some philosophers reveal an apparent commitment to a metaphysically robust understanding of information and information processing that is problematic. Consider, as an example, this passage from Chalmers:

I understand information in more or less the sense of Shannon (1948). Where there is information there are informational states embedded in an information space. . . . An information space is an abstract object, but following Shannon we can see information as physically embodied when there is a space of distinct physical states, the differences between which can be transmitted down some causal pathway. The transmittable states can be seen as themselves constituting an information space. . . . Physical information is a difference that makes a difference. (2010, p. 25)

Taken at its word, the idea expressed in this quotation is that "differences" between physical states are literally transmitted by causal means. But Chalmers also tells us that "states themselves" are transmittable—and that, because of this, physical information makes a difference. The passage presents a number of interpretative difficulties. Is physical information equated with differences between physical states? Is it the physical states themselves, or the differences between them, or both, that are somehow transmitted causally and that make a difference?

For those who want to understand how informational content "flows," a better answer (foreshadowed in our first chapter) calls on the vehicle/content distinction. This allows one to hold that informational content is not literally a kind of commodity that gets moved about and modified in various ways. Information-carrying vehicles are manipulated in various ways, but informational content never is; the latter—despite the metaphors—is not "like a parcel in the mail" (Shapiro 2011, p. 35). If this is accepted, bona fide cognitive systems cannot be special because they literally use and manipulate informational content (even with the provision that they do not understand such content). At best, they are special because it is their function to convey informational content without manipulating it as such.

We are now getting down to brass tacks. For this story to work, there must at least be content that these subsystems have the special function to convey—there must be something that it is their function to say even if they don't understand what they are saying or what is said. But exactly what is informational content?

Dretske speaks about informational content as "the what-it-is-we-can-learn from a signal or message in contrast to how-much-we-can-learn" (1981, p. 47). He makes clear that he understands a signal's informational content to be propositional content of the *de re* variety.[5] Propositions or propositional contents have special properties—minimally, they are bearers of truth. Assuming that informational contents are propositional is presumably what allows Dretske to hold that when signals carry information to the senses they "[tell] us truly about another state of affairs" (p. 44). This is, of course, quite compatible with holding that informational content lacks full-fledged representational properties. One can hold that informational content is supplied by the senses, thus ruling out the possibility of error in such cases. Indeed, this shows why informational content is importantly different from, and does not by itself suffice for, representational content.

At this juncture, both traditional defenders of CIC, those who endorse classical cognitivism, and latter-day CECers, who posit action-oriented representations, face a dilemma. To be precise, all defenders of CIC who subscribe to an explanatory naturalism face a dilemma. Since so much hangs on this, it is worth going over familiar ground carefully in preparation for our argument.

In the opening passage of Dretske's 1981 book *Knowledge and the Flow of Information* we find the foundational statement of how to understand information-processing systems in a way that is required by any CIC that expresses a commitment to explanatory naturalism:

In the beginning there was information. The word came later. . . . Information (though not meaning) [is] an *objective commodity*, something whose generation, transmission and reception do not require or in any way presuppose interpretative processes. One is therefore given a framework for understanding how meaning can evolve, how genuine cognitive systems—those with the resources for interpreting signals, holding beliefs, acquiring knowledge—can develop out of *lower-order, purely physical, information-processing mechanisms*. . . . Meaning, and the constellation of mental attitudes that exhibit it, are manufactured products. The raw material is information. (p. vii, emphases added)

Explanatory naturalism seeks to satisfy what Wheeler (2005, p. 5) charmingly calls the *Muggle constraint*: "One's explanation of some phenomenon meets the Muggle constraint just when it appeals only to entities, states and processes that are wholly nonmagical in character. In other words, no spooky stuff." It is widely supposed that the informational theory of content comfortably and easily meets this constraint. At least, its defenders have attempted to convince us that, when promoting it, there is nothing up their sleeves. This is because

the relevant notion of information at stake in informational semantics is the notion involved in many areas of scientific investigation as when it is said that a footprint or a fingerprint carries information about the individual whose footprint or fingerprint it is. In this sense, it may also be said that a fossil carries information about a past organism. The number of tree rings in a tree trunk carries information about the age of the tree. (Jacob 1997, p. 45, emphasis added)

Here the relevant notion of information is picked out by means of examples. We can call it information-as-covariance. Although theorists quibble about the strength and scope of the degree of covariance required in order for informational relations to exist, there is consensus that s's being F "carries information about" t's being H iff the occurrence of these states of affairs covary lawfully, or reliably enough.

But anything that deserves to be called content has special properties—e.g., truth, reference, implication—that make it logically distinct from, and not reducible to, mere covariance relations holding between states of affairs. Though covariance is surely scientifically respectable, it isn't able to do the required work of explaining content.

Put otherwise, if information is nothing but covariance then it is not any kind of content—at least, it is not content defined, even in part, in terms of truth-bearing properties. The number of a tree's rings can covary with the age of the tree; however, this doesn't entail that the first state of affairs says or conveys anything true about the second, or vice versa. The same goes for states that happen to be inside agents and which reliably correspond with external states of affairs—these too, in and of themselves, don't "say" or "mean" anything just in virtue of instantiating covariance relations.

In yet other words, it is important to distinguish the notion of information-as-covariance from its richer cousin semantic or intentional information—the kind of contentful information (the message) that some communications convey. (See Griffiths 2001 and Godfrey-Smith 2007.) Call this *information-as-content*. Naturalistic theories with explanatory ambitions cannot simply help themselves to the notion of information-as-content, since that would be to presuppose rather than explain the existence of semantic or contentful properties.

Quite generally, covariation in and of itself neither suffices for nor otherwise constitutes or confers content, where content minimally requires the existence of truth-bearing properties. Call this the Covariance Doesn't Constitute Content Principle. This principle undermines the assumption that covariation is any kind of content. There is no doubt that the idea of information-as-covariance is widely used in the sciences; hence, it is not a hostage to fortune for explanatory naturalists. But if the Covariance Doesn't Constitute Content Principle is true, there is a gaping explanatory hole in the official story propounded by those who follow Dretske's lead. Anyone peddling such an account is surely violating the Muggle constraint and ought to be brought to the attention of the Ministry of Magic.[6]

One might opt to be impaled on the first horn of the dilemma and retain the scientifically respectable notion of information-as-covariance. This would allow one to retain full naturalistic credentials while relinquishing the idea there is such a thing as informational content—the path we recommend. Note, however, that it requires giving up on CEC, since, as we argued in the preceding section, the minimal requirement for distinguishing information-*processing* systems from information-*sensitive* systems is that the former make use of action-oriented representations that are defined as content-bearing vehicles. But the distinction between vehicles and contents falls apart, at this level, if there are no informational contents to bear. To avoid the collapse of that distinction, one might opt to be impaled on the dilemma's second horn. Taking this option requires accepting that contentful properties exist even if they don't reduce to, or cannot be wholly explained in terms of, covariance relations. If contentful properties and covariance properties are logically distinct, they can still be systematically related. Hence, it might be hoped that contentful properties can be naturalistically explained by some other means (e.g., by some future physics). Alternatively, they could be posited as explanatory primitives—as metaphysical extras that might be externally related to covariance properties. Thus, they might have the status that Chalmers (2010) still assigns to qualia—they might require us to expand our understanding of the scope of the natural. Contentful properties might pick out properties that—like phenomenal properties—exist alongside, but can't be reduced to, basic physical properties. If that were the case, the explanatory project of naturalism with respect to them would be quite different—it would be to discover the set of fundamental bridging laws that explain how contentful properties relate to basic physical properties. That would be the only way to solve what we might call the Hard Problem of Content.

Of course, one might try to avoid both horns of the dilemma by demonstrating the falsity of the Covariance Doesn't Constitute Content Principle by showing how contentful properties—e.g., truth-bearing properties—reduce to covariance properties. The problem with this response is that the only (so far) developed line of reply that would make it plausible requires abandoning physicalism, so the metaphysical costs will be too heavy for most. (We discuss this in further detail in chapter 6.)

Of course, another way to avoid the dilemma would be to show that the required notion of information is meatier than covariance but is nonetheless equally naturalistically respectable. It might be thought that a candidate has already been identified. Dretske talks of indication relations, not covariance relations, though the two are often confused. Tellingly, after the passage cited above, Jacobs remarks: "In all of these cases, it is not unreasonable to assume that the informational relation holds between an indicator and what it indicates (or a source) independently of the presence of an agent with propositional attitudes." (1997, p. 45, emphasis added) In making this last point, Jacob recognizes that "the information or indication relation is going to be a relation between states or facts" (pp. 49–50).

However, following Grice, Dretske is wont to think of indication as natural meaning—as in "smoke means fire." But one can make an advance on the pure notion of covariance by assuming that smoke *means* fire only if it indicates fire to someone. Here indication implies the presence of a user. Indication is, at least, a three-place relation unlike covariance. To think in terms of information-as-indication as just defined is, therefore, to go beyond the covariance notion of information.[7]

Notice that the notion of information-as-indication already brings in more than the notion of information-as-covariance. But it is not at all clear that what it brings in can or should be identified with content. Still, even if we were to allow—for the sake of argument—that it *somehow* brings content into the picture, we would need full details about how this occurs to be confident of its naturalistic credentials. Until these questions are answered, CIC accounts (including CEC accounts that appeal to action-oriented representations)—which rely on the existence of informational content to distinguish bona fide cognitive systems from all others—are revealed to have feet of clay.

The "code" metaphor is rife in the cognitive sciences, but the cost of taking it seriously is that one must face up to the Hard Problem of Content. In light of the highlighted problems for CIC stories, we have reason to think that on-line sensory signals "carry information" in the covariance sense but not that they "pass on" meaningful or contentful messages. There is no naturally occurring contentful information that can be "used and fused" to form inner representations. Unless we assume that pre-existing contents exist to be received through sensory contact, the last thread of the analogy between basic cognitive systems and genuinely communicating systems breaks down at a crucial point.

In line with REC, there are alternative ways to understand cognitive activity as involving a complex series of systematic—but not contentfully mediated—interactions between well-tuned mechanisms. If they succeed, the above arguments should encourage more cautious CEC types—those trying to occupy the middle ground—to take a walk on the wild side.

Enactivist Makeovers

In this section we aim to show how, after a few well-motivated adjustments, existing theories of content begin to agree with radical enactivism: all roads lead to REC.

Teleofunctionalism

The foregoing discussion reveals that if we stick to the notion of information-as-covariance there are no grounds for thinking that the world, standing apart from agentive systems, contains anything that could be called informational *content*. If covariation is assumed to be the only worldly source of informational content, then, in light of the Covariance Doesn't Constitute Content Principle, we have, as yet, no explanation for the natural occurrence of informational content in the world.[8]

But what if we add information-exploiting organisms—beings that respond to the information in signals—to the picture? Might not content enter the story at this point? Perhaps the relevant work of explaining contentful responding might be shouldered by attending to the way information is used or consumed. Isn't this the main moral of Dretske's (1988) teleo-functional account of representation? It accepts that, although a tree's rings carry information (understood in the covaria-tional sense) about the tree's age, more is needed if there is to be representational content. As Currie reminds us, "a fallen tree bough may be pressed into service as a representation of the tree's age; then it is a representation because it is *used* to represent" (2010, p. 5).

Consider Dretske's own example. Stickleback, he observes, "exploit rather crude indicators (a bright red underside, for instance) to recognize one another," and "males use the bright red underside to identify male intruders, females use it to identify interested males" (1988, p. 103). This being so, "the fish react similarly to a variety of objects of similar coloration: painted bits of wood elicit aggressive behaviour in the males and sexual interest in the females. But in the fish's natural habitat the correlation is good enough. By and large, only stickleback have this coloration." (p. 103)

A teleofunctionalist would hold that certain internal states of the fish represent *because* they have the function to say how things stand with the world. Such states, which are thought to possess semantic content, are consumed by mechanisms within the fish that use them to guide the behavior of the fish in specified ways. Accordingly, the contents of such states are bossy. Not only do they tell organisms how things stand with the world (how it is); they also tell them what they should do given that things are that way.

In light of the argument in the preceding section, assessment of Dretske's teleofunctional proposal as a basis for a theory of content has to be handled with care. The crucial thing to note is that adding informationally sensitive users or consumers of information to the story leaves covariance relations unaltered; they remain just what they are and where they are. They are not converted into naturally occurring contentful relations by the addition of users that exploit them for certain purposes. For example, no informational content is "picked up" or "extracted from" the world and then "supplied" to the user by sensory means. Thus, the users' senses, in responding in informationally sensitive ways, do not convey any informational content to hypothesized internal cognitive mechanisms, thus telling them about the state of the world. Logic dictates that, if there is no informational content in the world, then there is no informational content in the world *to be acquired by minds*. To keep things straight, let's call this the No Acquired Content principle for short.

The No Acquired Content principle is bad news for any theory that thinks that informational content is the raw material of mental consumption—e.g., a kind of given that is literally furnished by the senses. The principle undermines any theory of representation that requires taking very seriously the idea that informational content is the basis for the production of more complex representations.

If we abandon the idea that cognition is essentially the construction of representations formed from informational contents, different explanatory avenues regain their proper importance. We can begin to attend to the details of what goes on in perception without gross oversimplification because we are devoting our energies, mistakenly, to trying to understand "the manner in which [sensory experience] codes information" (Dretske 1981 p. 146).

As we have seen, we must let go of the familiar notion that the primary role of informationally sensitive activity is to yield contentful, representational products. To some this might seem like a loss, but the gain of doing so is that it allows us to give due attention to the features of basic cognitive activity itself, which had been systematically and wrongly pushed into the background.

Shifting our focus in this way enables us to concentrate on how organisms respond to "higher-order invariants in a temporal series of signals—the kind of information [they] are able to [respond to] by moving around and registering systematic alterations in patterns, textures, and relative positions" (Dretske 1981, p. 145). This involves nothing less than understanding how "signals specifying the position of the head in relation to gravity, the angular position and movement of the eyes in relation to the head, and the relative position and movement of all other relevant body parts play a role in determining how we experience what we experience" (p. 146). In short, to get free of the standard CIC picture and put all of the complex dynamics required for cognition center stage is to effect an enactivist makeover.

Teleosemantics

For all that has been said, there is an obvious reply proponents of CIC can make. To promote their account, CICers need not posit informational contents that are conveyed via the senses and furnish the mind. Considerations about the function or *purpose* of information-sensitive responding might suffice to persuade us that, at least in some cases, such responding—in and of itself—qualifies as and thus constitutes a kind of contentful representing. This idea gets its most developed expression in the work of Millikan (1984, 1993, 2004). As she makes clear, according to her consumer-based theory of content, "the content of a representation is determined, in a *very important part*, by the systems that interpret it" (2005, p. 100, emphasis added).

Taking an even stronger line on this would involve holding that the interpretative response does *all* the work. This would surrender any commitment to the idea that informational content exists independently of the activities of cognitive agents.

What we call a Strengthened Millikan Maneuver is a promising strategy for other reasons too. It provides a clean way of avoiding the indeterminacy of content that plagues two-tiered teleofunctional accounts of the sort that Dretske (1988) propounds.[9]

Dretske's information-based teleofunctionalism is pulled in different directions in trying to decide what determines the content of a given representation. Is it the informational content of the natural indicator or the teleofunction of that indicator—the function that the indicator is meant to perform for the system—that determines an inner state's representational content? Is it what is reliably indicated or what the organism needs that decides the issue? This tension is much discussed. The standard solution is to lean on consumers' needs to fix representational content. Ryder (2006, p. 121) exemplifies this: "Although a tire gauge carries information about pressure, temperature and volume, it represents only pressure because that is what it is *supposed* to carry information about." If teleofunctions are sufficient to fix representational content, then it appears that any appeal to the information relations—along with the assumption that information is a kind of content—is superfluous for that task. This observation, in conjunction with the Covariance Doesn't Constitute Content Principle and the No Acquired Content Principle, gives reason to prefer a pure teleofunctional approach to content over one that depends on the pre-existence of informational content. But in taking this road one must relinquish the informational theory of content as a means of fixing content. According to teleosemantics, the responses of organisms carry all of the weight in performing that task.

Defenders of CIC may not see what all the fuss is about. After all, teleosemantic proposals are the clear front-runners among existing naturalistic proposals that seek to supply something more than covariance in order to explain representing. Teleose-mantics promises an account of the representational properties of mental states by focusing on how such states enable responses to aspects of environments in ways that answer organismic needs.

The guiding idea of this theory of content is that a device will have the teleofunction of representing Xs if it is used, inter-preted, or consumed by the system because it has the proper function of representing the presence of Xs. Talk of proper func-tion is meant to emphasize that content is fixed by what organ-isms are supposed to do in their interpretative activity rather than what they are merely disposed to do. Despite the normative language, the intention is to explain representational properties in wholly naturalistic terms—for example, by appealing to stan-dards set by natural selection and by individual learning and training.

The trouble, once again, is that the metaphors mislead. If we adopt the Strengthened Millikan Maneuver, we can't think of cognitive agents as content-using, content-consuming, or con-tent-interpreting systems, for to do so suggests that there is pre-existing content to be dealt with. In any case, such thinking is not an adequate construal of the commitments of teleoseman-tics, since, as Cummins et al. (2006) observes, the latter "requires selection to pre-date content" (p. 199).

Those who endorse the strengthened Millikan maneuver should speak of content-creating systems and not of content-consuming systems. That's an important step in the right direc-tion, but note, now, how much this account begins to look like the enactivist story we want to tell.

Some enactivists have acknowledged the need to augment their basic framework with more robust biological notions. For example, according to Di Paolo (2009, p. 12) "it is a mistake to take the theory of autopoiesis as originally formulated as a finished theory. . . . Autopoiesis leaves many questions unanswered. In particular, several essential issues that could serve as a bridge between mind and life (like a proper grounding of teleology and agency) are given scant or null treatment in the primary literature."

Addressing this concern, Thompson maintains that "cognition is behavior in relation to meaning and norms that the system itself enacts or brings forth on the basis of its autonomy" (2007, p. 126, emphases added). He posits "virtual milieus," "vital norms," and meaning as essential features of cognition. He notes that even bacterial cells—the simplest life forms on earth (where life is understood autopoietically)—have needs that are fulfilled by deriving nutrition from the environment. They achieve their ends by ingesting sucrose—an environmental feature. Thompson holds that the property of being a nutrient is a virtual property, not something found "objectively" in the environment. Rather, "it is enacted or brought forth by the way the organism, given its autonomy and the norms its autonomy brings about, couples with the environment" (2007, p. 74). Thus, "sucrose has meaning and value as food but only in the milieu that 'the system itself brings into existence' or 'constitutes for itself'" (p. 74). The whole point of Thompson's enactivism is that behavior "expresses meaning-constitution rather than information processing" (p. 71). This reveals the evident similarities between strengthened teleosemantics and Autopoietic Enactivism. In a similar fashion REC can make use of some resources from a suitably modified teleosemantics.

Talk of "enacting meanings" and "vital norms" will seem alien, or misplaced, to many analytic philosophers, but it should help that Thompson makes it quite clear that he is concerned with norms in "the biological sense" (2007, p. 75). This is evident from the fact that the "meaning" and the "value" in question neither constitute semantic contents nor depend on such content for their existence. For this reason, Thompson insists that "if we wish to continue using the term representation, then we need to be aware of what sense this term can have for the enactive approach. . . . Autonomous systems do not operate on the basis of internal representations. . . . They enact an environment." (ibid., pp. 58–59). Substantively we agree, but it only breeds confusion to use terms like 'meaning' and 'representation' to describe the cognitive antics of bacteria. We prefer the more austere talk of informationally sensitive responses to natural signs. Thankfully, if all this is right, we don't need theories of mental content in order to understand basic forms of intentional directedness. Nothing important is lost if we put teleosemiotics in the place of teleosemantics. Teleosemiotics is (basically) teleosemantics without the semantic ambitions.

Teleosemiotics

Teleosemiotics borrows what is best from teleosemantics to provide a content-free, naturalistic account of the determinate kinds of intentional directedness that organisms exhibit toward aspects of their environments. Yet, unlike teleosemantics, it does not seek to understand the most basic forms of directedness in semantic, contentful, or representational terms. It holds that the biologically basic modes of organismic responding don't involve content, where content is understood in terms of either reference, truth, or accuracy. Teleosemiotics is simply the logical fallout of rejecting the ambition to understand basic responding in representationalist terms while keeping the remainder of the teleosemantic apparatus.

The real point of conflict between what is on offer from REC and what is on offer from teleosemanticists is the commitment to content. How should we decide the issue? Invoking her favorite example, bee dances, Millikan describes the thought that drives her representationalist proposal:

> What makes the dances into representations is not what they do but why they work, why they help to cause arrival at sites of nectar, hence the arrival of nectar in the hive, hence well-fed larval bees. They work by bearing a correspondence to what they represent. . . . Why is this intentionality? Because the dances *display the characteristic trait of the intentional; namely they can be wrong or false.* . . . Should anything disturb the normal mapping between the shape of the dance and the location of the nectar, this misalignment will, quite literally lead the workers astray. Bee dances *have truth-conditions.* (2005, p. 97, emphases added)

There is, however, a well-known technical problem for Millikan's proposal. Compelling arguments show that it can, at best, account for states of mind exhibiting intentional (with a 't') directedness but it flounders when it comes to accounting for states of mind exhibiting intensionality (with an 's')—and the latter are required for having truth-evaluable thoughts.

Fodor (1990) observed that selectionist explanations, like historical explanations, are transparent (i.e., extensional). If that is so, explanations in terms of proper functions couldn't possibly identify a description that unequivocally specified the content of some state of mind. The assumption that representational states of mind possess semantic (intensional) content runs into trouble because biology lacks the resources for specifying under which guise such states might represent what they target.

The best response to Fodor's objection is to insist that content is determined by the needs of the consumer. Unpacking this idea requires looking at what—in the historical environment—shaped the organism's devices in order to determine what current descendants of those devices are meant to target. Accordingly, the semantic contents of representations are fixed by what in fact originally promoted the continued proliferation of devices that were "selected for." This sort of reply, championed by Millikan (1993), nevertheless misses its mark. It appears only to enable us to decide what a particular sort of device or response would have had to target, extensionally speaking, in the historical environment. But that doesn't address Fodor's real worry. Even if we can specify what is meant to be targeted that would give us exactly no reason to think that the targeted item is represented in a truth-conditional, referential, or otherwise semantic way—i.e., that it has intensional content. Thus, as Fodor highlights, his objection concerns not the tension "between the Darwinism and theories that are intentional (with a 't') but the tension between Darwinism and theories that are intensional (with an 's')" (2008a, p. 1).

There are positive lessons to learn from this polemic. With important adjustments, much can be salvaged from attempts to naturalize representational content. For example, although teleosemantic accounts fail to provide an adequate basis for naturalizing intensional content, they provide adequate tools for making sense of something more modest—i.e., responses involving only intentionality.

With this in mind it is useful to note that even those who were initially optimistic about the prospects of teleosemantics have come to doubt that such theories have any chance of success in achieving their stated aims of providing properly semantic theories of mental content. Godfrey-Smith (2006, p. 42) provides an astute assessment: "There is a growing suspicion that we have been looking for the wrong kind of theory, in some big sense. Naturalistic treatments of semantic properties have somehow lost proper contact with the phenomena." But Godfrey-Smith also acknowledges that the driving idea behind teleosemantics—that evolved structures can have a kind of "specificity" or "directedness"—is essentially correct: "[T]here is an important kind of natural involvement relation that is picked out by selection-based concepts of function. But this relation is found in many cases that do not involve representation or anything close to it." (ibid., p. 60)

In short, it is becoming clear to many in the field that purely biologically based accounts lack the right resources for naturalizing mental states with properly semantic properties, such as truth and reference. If we reject teleosemantics in favor of teleosemiotics, we can borrow what is best from the former as well as accepting covariance accounts of information in order to provide a content-free naturalistic account of the determinate intentional directedness that organisms exhibit toward aspects of their environments (Hutto 2008, chapter 3). All this requires is abandoning the attempt to understand the most basic forms of directedness in semantic, representational terms—in terms of contentful states of mind that exhibit properties of reference, truth, or accuracy. This is to accept that organisms often act successfully by making appropriate responses to objects or states of affairs in ways that are only mediated by their sensitive responding to natural signs, where this responding does not involve contentfully representing the objects or states of affairs in question.

As the Rolling Stones sang, "You can't always get what you want, but if you try sometimes you just might find you get what you need." Teleosemantic accounts do not provide an adequate basis for naturalizing semantic or intensional content, but they are proceeding along the right lines. Crucially, with a major adjustment to their aspirations, they provide serviceable tools for making sense of something more modest: organismic responses involving intentionality.

A truly radical enactivism—REC—holds that it is possible to explain a creature's capacity to perceive, keep track of, and act appropriately with respect to some object or property without positing internal structures that function to represent, refer to, or stand for the object or property in question. Our basic ways of responding to worldly offerings are not semantically content-ful. Still, it is possible to explain how perception gets its work done in guiding cognitive activity—even when it is quite sophis-ticated—without assuming the truth of CIC. RECers can still endorse the idea that organisms are informationally sensitive (i.e., that they exploit correspondences in their environments to adaptively guide their actions) while denying that it follows that they take in, store, or process informational content.

Linguistically grounded beliefs and judgments are, undoubt-edly, semantically contentful. Nevertheless, we conjecture that the great bulk of world-directed, action-guiding cognition exhib-its intentional directedness that is not contentful in the sense just discriminated. It is possible that even sophisticated forms of human visual perceiving are not essentially contentful or rep-resentational. The next two chapters further motivate this idea.

5 CIC's Retreat

Honorable retreats are no ways inferior to brave charges, as having less fortune, more of discipline, and as much valor.
—William Orville Douglas

Falling Back to High Ground

So far, we have considered the standard reasons for thinking that very basic forms of cognition must be CIC and have reviewed proposals about how they could be so. We have found both the reasons and the supporting proposals wanting. Up to now, REC has been pitted against unrestricted CIC—the idea that CIC is true of all forms of cognition. Against this idea we have argued that CIC's explanatory apparatus is both inappropriate and unnecessary: it fails to account for many highly sophisticated, intentionally directed and engaged doings—not only the doings of certain artificial agents and insects, but also many human doings, including reachings and graspings.

In the course of making our case against CEC (CIC's best champion in this arena), we exposed a devastating problem that all friends of unrestricted CIC must face up to: the Hard Problem of Content. Thus, we have reached a pivotal point. For without a solution to the Hard Problem of Content, the ambitions of those who hope to show that REC is wholly false by invoking the Information-Processing Challenge are thwarted. Indeed, unless that problem is solved there appear to be excellent reasons for favoring REC accounts of basic cognition in this domain over their CIC competitors, including CEC. If these arguments are sound, the best move that diehard friends of CIC can make at this juncture is to attempt a strategic retreat. They can try to hold a strong line against REC only by drawing it further back. Retreat is not defeat. CICers might cut their losses, fall back, and secure a more defensible position. Advocates of CIC might admit that it has no business trying to explain the kinds of doings on which the dispute has focused so far. In pressing for a modestly restricted CIC they could either simply concede that explanatory ground to REC or, less plausibly, return to an option floated briefly in chapter 3 and stipulate that—despite its complexities—the kinds of on-line activity in question don't require cognitive explanations at all, because they don't warrant CIC explanations.

Either way, a modestly restricted CIC agrees with REC that, when it comes to explaining and grounding content, all existing naturalized theories are "dispensable, redundant, and misleading" (Burge 2010, p. 9).[1] Burge, who adopts this restricted CIC line, agrees that no one should have ever expected that the sorts of theories discussed in chapter 4 could have carried the day in accounting for bona fide representational content. His verdict is tied to the observation that "information, correlation, causation, function, and so on are not distinctively psychological terms" (ibid., p. 9). By Burge's lights, the attempt to account for contentful representation in these deflationary (i.e., reductively naturalistic) terms was always doomed to fail (or, at least, destined to tacitly change the subject by positing only contentless representations, a move which appears oxymoronic).

The fallback move yields a crucial advantage—at least potentially: it allows proponents of CIC to avoid the Hard Problem of Content. However, there is a price to be paid for adopting this strategy. Ultimately, it requires grounding and motivating belief in an appropriately strong account of content in some other way—i.e., by appealing to something other than deflationary theories of content. A different account of content—derived from a different source—is needed. This requires either providing a robust alternative theory of content or—in *lieu* of that— at least a compelling motivation for believing that a modestly restricted CIC applies anyway.

Where to draw the line? Those who hold that basic minds are essentially contentful hope to protect CIC's fortunes by insisting, in a principled way, that the lower border of mind is located in a different place than has been supposed so far. Negatively, they must insist that, if it turns out to be possible to account for some seemingly intelligent activity adequately using nothing more than deflationary resources, CIC isn't needed to explain the activity. This provides a negative criterion for what is distinctively psychological and truly mental. To put this another way, for CICers of this persuasion the only notion of representation that theories of the deflationary stripe could legitimately supply is too weak to be capable of dealing with the sorts of explananda that demand CIC explanantia. By these lights, deflationary accounts might, at best, explain "mere awareness of sensations or merely reflexive sensitivities that connect with the environment in ways that satisfy the individual's needs" (Burge 2010, p. 7).

Modestly restricted CIC are interested in richer explananda. They are concerned only with the sorts of phenomena that cannot possibly be explained without an account of how individuals represent aspects of the world objectively—i.e., as being in a specific way that may not obtain. Although the tactic of strategic retreat gives these CICers a fighting chance, they must take care not to restrict their ambitions too much, to retreat too far. Otherwise they will be committed to the incredible view that there really isn't much cognition about at all. This result would follow, for example, if both CIC were true of all bona fide cognition and it turned out that it was only necessary to invoke genuinely representational contents in order to explain the sorts of cognition related to and dependent upon the use of language.

We are attracted to the view that it is appropriate and necessary to speak of contentful attitudes in such cases; this is where CIC has real explanatory purchase. But it is precisely because we think CIC is limited to such cases that we reject a standard that requires minds to be contentfully representational as being the sole—or the best—standard for determining what falls under the categories of "cognitive" or "minded" in general. There are other forms of bona fide cognition. For those hoping to challenge REC accepting that representational minds only come onto the scene along with language use would be to defend an overly restricted CIC.

Consequently, to have an interesting stake in this debate, defenders of a modestly restricted CIC must defend the view that the most elementary kind of mind—that with representational content—appears neither too low nor too high in the order of things. The explanatory target of a modestly restricted CIC must be just so. On the one hand, it must be something more than the kinds of capacities that can be understood wholly in terms of informational covariance and biological functionality. On the other hand, it must not be restricted only to cognitive capacities associated with and dependent upon the mastery of complex language.

In this light, perception and perceptual experience fit the bill perfectly. Many find it intuitive that perceptual states of mind entail and must be accounted for in terms of representational content. Moreover, it is arguable that perceptual activity of a putatively representational sort sits neatly between the kinds of on-line responding described in chapter 3 and the sorts of cognition associated with full-blown linguistic content. Surely if perceptual experiences do possess representational content inherently they do so quite independently and autonomously of linguistic capacities. Given this, it is not surprising that proponents of a modestly restricted CIC choose this ground upon which to make a credible last stand.

REC, in contrast, holds that, although in perception there is a certain way that the world is phenomenally experienced, such experiencing is not intrinsically contentful. Perceptual experiences can incline or prompt explicitly contentful beliefs and judgments, but they do not, in and of themselves, attribute properties to the world. Consequently, they do not have built-in conditions of satisfaction, nor do they possess veridical content that is accurate or inaccurate, true or false. If basic perceptual experiences—even those of the phenomenally conscious sort—possess no content, then there is simply no question of their being true or false, veridical or unveridical.

Friends of CIC must deny the possibility of contentless perceiving and defend the view that perceiving constitutes some kind of contentful attitude, even if the attitude in question turns out to be unlike other propositional attitudes in important respects. To do this, they must make a convincing case for the idea that perceiving is a type of contentful attitude that is quite distinct from—and comes before and below, both phylogenetically and ontogenetically—even the simplest kind of perceptual belief.

Obviously, those pursuing the modestly restricted CIC strategy of holding the line at perceptual experience must endorse intellectualism. But intellectualism comes in more expensive and less expensive forms, and some of these forms can be ruled out as unfit for duty at this point since they require the success of deflationary strategies—strategies that are not credible unless the Hard Problem of Content is answered or defused.

Consequently, to have any chance of success, modestly restricted CIC has to posit the least expensive forms of intellectualism about perceptual experience, since these have lighter explanatory burdens that don't necessitate having to deal with the Hard Problem of Content. Minimal intellectualists hold that perceptual experience is essentially representational, but they are not automatically committed to the existence of contentful representations of the sort that would have to be explained by appealing to failed, deflationary theories of content.

To clarify how light the commitments of minimal intellectualism can be, it is instructive to compare them with the commitments of hyperintellectualism. The latter, although pitched at the right explanatory level to do the work that a modestly restricted CIC requires, is unsuitable for the reasons just stated. However, systematically subtracting three of hyperintellectualism's main commitments converts it into a minimal intellectualism that can do the required work. The next two sections of this chapter show how this can be achieved through a process of theoretical adjustment. In the final section, we describe maximally minimal intellectualism, which goes a step further, reducing its understanding of what is necessary for there to be perceptual content by focusing on accuracy conditions as opposed to truth conditions. Maximally minimal intellectualism is REC's main and most interesting rival. It has the best chance of being true—and, if true, of defeating a REC account of perception and perceptual experience.

Having prepared the ground in this chapter, in the next chapter we will examine maximally minimal intellectualism more closely, arguing that when carefully scrutinized there are no compelling empirical or philosophical reasons to endorse such a view.

Hyperintellectualism

In line with a long-standing philosophical tradition, some hold not only that perceptual experiences are representational in and of themselves but also that perceptual representation is made possible only by other activities involving the manipulation of contents and representations. Galen Strawson helpfully highlights what we take to be the three canonical assumptions of the most extreme form of hyperintellectualism in the following passage:

You look out of your window, and you see an armoured personnel carrier rusting under a tree on the far side of the river. In such a case, you [1] *take up* in a spatially distributed array of color patches, whatever else you do. But the character of your experience is fundamentally determined by your sense of your position relative to other objects, [2] *your immediate and automatic judgments* of size, three-dimensional shape, and distance, and your equally immediate experience-conditioning [3] *deployment of specific concepts*, like the concepts of tree and water. . . . (1994, p. 4, emphases and labels added)

If Strawson is to be believed, a great deal of intellectual activity is required if an individual is to enjoy even the simplest of perceptual experiences. This is hyperintellectualism. Its commitments are most clearly elaborated in modern guise in Fodor's views on perception, as developed in his celebrated 1983 book *The Modularity of Mind* and in later writings. Fodor's position is blatantly hyperintellectualist: not only does he assume that perceptual experiences possess representational content; he insists that this is possible only because of the existence of many other kinds of mental representations.

For comparative purposes—in order to contrast this view with more minimal kinds of intellectualism—let us consider what Fodor has to say on this topic in some detail. Focusing on Fodor is a good choice not only because he provides the most developed and influential contemporary hyperintellectualist account on today's market, but also because he aspires to explain, in an entirely naturalistic fashion, how contentful perceptual representation of an objective world comes about by CIC means. This ambition helpfully throws the kinds of theoretical costs incurred for naturalists who adopt extreme hyperintellectualism into sharp relief. And doing so sets the stage for showing how such costs can be avoided by adopting hyperintellectualism's much less spendthrift (and ultimately much more plausible) cousin, minimal intellectualism, which we will describe in the next section.

Giving just the barest bones of the view, Fodor tells us that "any mechanism whose states covary with environmental ones can be thought of as registering information about the world; and given the satisfaction of certain further conditions, the output of such systems can be reasonably thought of as representations of the environmental states with which they covary" (1983,

p. 39). Registering information might mean no more than an individual's being in an internal state that lawfully covaries with some environmental one. That reading is not controversial. It is only when registration is understood in combination with other claims about the nature of what perceptual excavation involves that it becomes so. For example, Fodor holds that even the initial stages of perceptual processing involve the uptake of nonconceptualized contents—contents that he deems to be representational in a special, limited sense. Indeed, such content is "taken up" in experience supplying the core content of perception, even though that content does not become representational in a more robust sense until further stages of representationally based processing occur and until concepts are applied to it.

By Fodor's lights, to be in a state that registers information is simply to be in a state that contains Dretskian information about some other state. Even so, Fodor maintains that being in such a state suffices to "represent" another state of affairs merely by carrying information about it. But since representing a state of affairs by carrying information about it is transparent to coreferential substitution of identicals, it follows that what we are allegedly dealing with in such cases is at best a form of "representation that's not 'under a description'" (Fodor 2008b p. 179).[2] Given this, it is possible "to register the Dretskian information that a is F even if you don't have the concept F" (p. 186). As Fodor sees it, all this adds up to the claim that registering is a kind of nonconceptual representing—albeit of a sort that is distinct from and more basic than representing *as*.

Now, it might not be obvious how—even if we allow that there is nonconceptual representation here that involves only informational content—informational content of this sort has anything to do with what is taken up or given in perceptual *experience*, such as the arrays of color patches of which Strawson speaks.

The final link connecting Fodor's account to Strawson's first condition requires appreciating that Fodor thinks that what allegedly is "taken up" in the first stage of perceptual processing is not only contentful but also experiential. This is to equate Dretskian informational content with experiential content. Fodor (2008b, p. 180) makes this equation, albeit without providing an account of how or why we should believe in such an identity. Nevertheless, what is on offer is an account of a nonconceptual, contentful experiential given—a notion that plays a pivotal part if it is the work of concepts to "recover from experience the information that it contains" (ibid., p. 181).

According to this brand of hyperintellectualism, registering is understood as a means of supplying experiential raw material for perceiving proper. In the initial stages of perceptual processing, content is registered and received by the senses. It is subsequently modified by a series of intellectually driven, representationally informed operations before concepts are brought to bear on it. This is the first point at which content enters into the hyperintellectualist story.

The next stage of processing, hyperintellectualists assume, does the work of Strawson's immediate and automatic judgments. These "judgments," which also allegedly make perceiving possible, entail the existence of content. In Fodor's version such judgments are nothing other than the inferences made by perceptual modules. Modules are conceived of as domain-specific cognitive devices that receive inputs (transduced informational contents "supplied" by the senses) and perform intellectual operations upon such contents—operations such as analysis and inference. Fodor (1983, p. 42) makes this clear when he talks of the "inferences" at issue having "as their 'premises' transduced representations of proximal stimulus configurations, and as their 'conclusions' representations of the character and distribution of distal objects."

The principles involved in such inferring are literally embedded in modules; such principles are, in fact, represented in and by the system, and are fully propositional and conceptually grounded. Because of this, the existence of such background laws and principles entails the existence of sub-personal, sub-doxastic "innately cognized propositional contents" (ibid., p. 5). The domain-specific principles that enable modules to do their analyzing work are assumed to be fully represented, if only tacitly, by the system. Hence, they need not be cognitively or consciously accessible to their users. Nevertheless, if such principles exist, it must be explained how they be can be contentful.

Not only are hyperintellectualists committed to the existence of contentful givens and representations of the relevant perceptual formation principles; they also take it for granted that specific concepts must inform what is given in experience if experiences are to have their particular, world-referring, objective content. Like other hyperintellectualists, Fodor takes it that to perceptually represent also necessarily involves subsuming unconceptualized representational contents under some concepts, for to represent X *as F* necessarily requires mastery and deployment of the concept F.

Concepts, it is typically assumed, have intensions that denote classes of things with determinate extensions—i.e., that to have the concept of X is to have a contentful mental representation that picks out all and only Xs. Thus concepts are "mental representations of a sort that can occur in thought. Thoughts are composed of concepts" (Tye 2009, p. 40).

Promoters of hyperintellectualism insist that conceiving is necessary for perceiving. Consequently, if one assumes that perceptual experiencing is widespread throughout the animal kingdom, it follows that the members of many, many animal species are concept users. This is accepted without qualm by those who defend the view that even some invertebrates, such as ants and honeybees, operate with concepts. Carruthers unashamedly writes:

Consider, for example, a honeybee's thought with the content [nectar is 200 meters north of the hive] (or some near equivalent). Is this genuinely composed of the concepts nectar, 200 meters (or some roughly equivalent measure of distance), north (or some similar solar-based measure of direction), and hive? Well, yes. (2009, p. 98)

In the light of these three commitments, it is clear that hyperintellectualism is an expensive view. By assuming that contentful perceiving cannot occur without the company of many other kinds of mental representations, it runs up a hefty explanatory bill. Without an answer to the Hard Problem of Content, there is every reason to doubt that this bill can be covered. As we argued in the preceding chapter, no satisfactory answer is provided by the standard naturalized theories of content—i.e., those that appeal to properties such as causation, nomic covariation, and/or biological function.[3] Thus, any brand of hyperintellectualism that has aspirations of being explanatorily naturalistic faces a serious if not utterly crippling challenge.

Minimal Intellectualism

There is another way to go. One can endorse a robust representationalism about perceptual experience while relinquishing all the problematic hyperintellectualist commitments mentioned above. By systematically relinquishing these commitments as unnecessary, minimal intellectualism might appear to avoid hyperintellectualism's cul de sac while still making sufficient room for the idea that perceptual states (or activities) are essentially contentful and representational.

A first step in the direction of minimal intellectualism is to deny that perceiving depends on "taking up" experiential, contentful givens. This is to abandon the idea that there is a kind of given—an informational or minimally representational content that is supplied by the senses.

The next step is to reject the idea that perceptual systems must literally represent their laws of operation, even if only by tacit subpersonal, subdoxastical means. Fodorian modules are defined as informationally encapsulated *cognitive* mechanisms, where cognitive mechanisms are definitively marked as having a representational basis. This dependence on representations is what distinguishes modules from mere domain-specific psychological mechanisms, as Fodor sees it. Indeed, Fodor insists that attributing propositional knowledge to subpersonal mechanisms is "*the* characteristic feature of contemporary cognitivist theorizing" (2001, p. 109, emphasis added).[4]

It is possible to hold that there are specialized perceptual devices—even devices inherited from a perceiver's evolutionary forebears—without assuming that such devices are cognitive in the sense that Fodor specifies. Such devices would not be modules in the strict sense, but they might nevertheless have the specialized task of handling responses to information such as is required for the formation of perceptual attitudes. One can accept this without assuming that the principles by which such devices operate are represented, at any level, in the devices themselves. Burge (2010, p. 405) makes this very clear:

An individual perceptual system no more implicitly represents laws determining, or principles governing, transformations of states than the
solar system implicitly represents Kepler's or Newton's laws. In both cases, the laws are real. In neither case are they represented by elements of
the subject matter governed by the laws. . . . To represent 'implicitly' the
laws determining perceptual transformations, the system would have to
have content representing not only the mathematical operations con-
tained in the laws. The system would also have to have contents that
represent the perceptual states and contents that the laws incorporate.
Perceptual systems do not have representational contents of, or as of,
their own states or operations, even 'implicitly'. To perceive, individuals
need not *represent* their own states or operations, even 'implicitly'.

(For similar assessments, see Hutto 2005 and chapter 3 of Hutto
2008.)

The final step in the move away from hyperintellectualism is
to abandon the idea that perceptual content must, always and
everywhere, be conceptually informed. There have been many
different nonconceptualist proposals—some stronger and some
weaker—since the possibility was first articulated by Dretske
(1981) and Evans (1982). Much ink has been spilled on this
topic.

The most modest version of nonconceptualism holds only
that at least some contents of experience outstrip conceptual
capacities, sometimes. This way of formulating the claim is consistent with holding, for example, that conceptual contents are
always necessary for perceptual experience, but that they don't
tell the whole story about its nature. On at least some occasions,
conceptual perceptual contents might be accompanied by nonconceptual perceptual contents.

The stronger and more usual claim advanced by most non-
conceptualists is that it is possible to have perceptual experiences without possessing the appropriate concepts (or without

actually applying them, if we assume that the perceiver possesses them or, at least, might come to possess them). The strongest view, which sits best with a properly minimal intellectualism, assumes that perceptual experience is possible in the complete absence of concepts. This might be further augmented by the claim that the very nature of such perceptual content debars the possibility of ever fully or exhaustively capturing its essence by means of conceptual, descriptive characterization.

In the absence of a clear and settled definition of the nature of concepts, several authors have noted that any proposal to the effect that perception exhibits nonconceptual content remains "vague" and ill defined (Stalnaker 1998; Gunther 2003). Though there is truth to that observation, it has implications for conceptualism too. Historically, the proposal that there might be nonconceptual perceptual content was made in response to the assumption that all perceptual content is conceptual. It was a reaction. The substance of any such claim depends on what theory of concepts is in play. If it turns out that there is no clear understanding of what concepts are, or of what is required for their possession and application, then proposals about how and where to draw the line between the conceptual and the nonconceptual are bound to be fuzzy. In this light, it should be clear that the concern about vagueness affects conceptualism and nonconceptualism alike. Moreover, noting that such vagueness exists provides no justification for thinking that conceptualism ought to be privileged as the default way of characterizing the content of perceptions.

A standard consideration that favors the idea that perceptual experiences must be nonconceptual—perhaps even essentially so in the strongest sense—is that the content of experiences exhibits a specificity that systematically eludes capture in any purely conceptual repertoire. In defending this view, Gauker (2011) articulates two assumptions that he takes to feature in any credible conceptualism. The first assumption—the Expressibility Assumption—states that "wherever there is conceptual content, there is the possibility of expressing that content in words—the words of a humanly possible language" (p. 60). The idea is not that the words needed to express the relevant concept will be already available, prêt-à-porter, but that they could, in principle, be tailored to requirements.

Adding to this, Gauker holds that if such words for expressing the relevant concepts were to be available then the perceiver should be able, *ceteris paribus*, to conceptually describe the contents of what they perceive without further ado—in particular, "without undertaking any empirical investigation into the nature of his or her perception" (ibid., p. 60). Fittingly, he calls this second assumption "the Accessibility Assumption."

With these two assumptions in hand, Gauker presents a dilemma for conceptualists about content. He offers them an exhaustive choice of vocabulary for capturing the allegedly conceptual content of perception. The first option is to rely on general predicates—such as 'chair'—that admit of various more specific sub-species, such as 'Windsor chair', 'Bubble chair', and 'bench'. The second and the only other strategy is to deploy maximally determinate predicates that pick out only a single species. Although the latter might admit of various instances, the concept does not sub-divide further into sub-species.

On this basis Gauker identifies what is, in effect, a problem of interpretation—one that plagues anyone attempting the first strategy, suggesting that there is simply no way to decide what the appropriate level of specificity is that is required to express the content of a perceptual experience. Going by the resources readily available to us, there is no principled way to decide which predicates the right description should include or exclude. Gauker cites the following example:

Suppose I am looking at a certain chair. It's a Windsor chair. It has arms. It is made of wood. So the candidates for the sentences that might express the content of my perception include predicates of a wide variety of criss-crossing levels of generality, such as:

That's a chair!
That's a Windsor chair!
That's a wooden armchair!
That's a wooden piece of furniture!
(2011, p. 62).

But the conceptualist fares no better by adopting the alternative technique—that of deploying some maximally determinate predicate. Gauker's criticism of this proposal is that this move fails just because there are no decent candidates for such predicates. If that is so, this tactic is a non-starter. Returning to the same case of being confronted with a particular chair, Gauker considers how one might try to express the imagined conceptual content of such an experience by using a maximally determinate predicate such as 'shape$_{55}$'. But, he wonders, what property might such a gerrymandered predicate denote (assuming, all the while, that the concepts of experience must pick out something external to and independent of the internal properties of the experiences themselves)?[5] As Gauker notes, things of many different sorts of shapes might appear under certain viewing conditions just as the currently viewed chair appears, and hence there is no unique shape that answers to any worldly property that 'shape$_{55}$' could pick out.

As long as the Expressibility and Accessibility assumptions are in play, it seems that conceptualism faces an apparently insurmountable problem: it can't specify the content of perceptions. This fact leads Gauker to endorse nonconceptualism of the strongest variety: "[T]here is no conceptual content of perception to express." (2011, p. 64). Thus, for him, the fact that it is possible to apply various concepts to perceptual experience fails to capture what is essential to the content of experience. That concepts can be brought to bear on the context of experience is "entirely incidental" (p. 150).

There are other routes to the same conclusion, even if we imagine that this problem might be overcome or avoided. There are arguments in favor of nonconceptualism even if we imagine there to be some perfect conceptual fit—one with just the right level of specificity—for each and every experienced property. Flouting Gauker's twin assumptions, one might imagine that some demonstrative concepts are always tacitly attributed by the visual system to each and every experienced property.[6] In such a case, it might be thought that the conceptual content of experience could be captured appropriately and exhaustively by a conjunction of such predicates. Such a conceptual content would be expressible, at least in principle, if we could but get at it.

Even if we don't question its conceivability, this is an incredible thesis. The idea that perceptual systems might be continually making such conceptual attributions, on the fly, looks deeply implausible when we consider the fact that there are "an indefinitely large number of relevant contextual features, and which features of the context are relevant will change from situation to situation" (Kelly 2001/2003, p. 229). To put it mildly, it would be difficult to explain how our visual systems can have the requisite cognitive resources and agility for making so many relevant conceptual assignments—and for updating these at such a remarkably quick pace.

Connected with this, a strong reason for thinking that perceptual contents are nonconceptual is that they exhibit a kind of situation dependence: "[P]erceptual experience of a property is always dependent upon . . . two aspects of the situation . . . context and object." (Kelly 2001/2003, p. 229)

In the light of these considerations, nonconceptualism about perceptual content is surely an attractive option. It spares us the need to address interpretative conundrums of the sort that Gauker highlights while saving us from having to explain how creatures can perceive complex visual scenes without, in effect, having to solve a kind of frame problem and suffering cognitive overload. Therefore, the idea that perceptual content might be essentially nonconceptual is not only a live possibility; for these and other reasons, it appears to be a good bet.

Maximally Minimal Intellectualism

Minimal intellectualism, as we define it, retains the idea that perception has truth-conditional content while denying (1) that the senses supply contentful givens, (2) that the principles of perceptions are represented by and within perceptual systems, and (3) that perceptual content is essentially conceptual.

Taking this limbo pole ("how low can you go?") strategy to a new level, maximally minimal forms of intellectualism reduce their CIC commitments further. Not only do they reject 1–3; they also deny that perceptual contents have to be truth-conditional contents. This latter move is motivated by, if not a logical consequence of, the abandonment of the third hyper-intellectualist thesis—i.e., that perceptual content is necessarily conceptually informed.

Maximally minimal intellectualism therefore rejects the intuition that if perception is representational then it must represent in a truth-evaluable way. Perceptual experience represents if and only if it takes some portion of the world to be a certain way; if it attributes properties to particulars. In the simplest cases this might take the form of attributions such as X's being hot or Y's being colored. Yet, since the world may not be as it is represented as being, it may seem to follow that any perceptual content must be straightforwardly true or false. To assume that is to assume that the content of perceptions is exactly the same kind of content that gets expressed in linguistic utterances, the same kind of content that is possessed by beliefs and judgments. When the debate about nonconceptual content began, little or no attention was given to the question of whether perceptual content, in virtue of being nonconceptual, might be incapable of being truth conditional. Nowadays it is widely agreed that nonconceptual content lacks the intensionality needed for there to be determinate truth conditions, and that only conceptual content has that intensionality. If that is so, it rules out the possibility that nonconceptual content might be truth conditional. If perceptual content is nonconceptual, then it is not propositional.

Of course, it does not follow that perceiving is contentless if not all content need be truth conditional. (See Gunther 2003, p. 5–6.) However, if perceiving is to have content then it must have conditions of satisfaction of some kind. This is the most general and the most minimal requirement on the existence of content.

Motivated by these considerations, the trend today is to press for the existence of nonconceptual content understood in a new fashion. Crane (2009), Burge (2010), and Gauker (2011) explicitly reject the propositional-attitude thesis about perception, but they do so without surrendering commitment to the idea that perceptual states are essentially representational. Rather, they maintain that perceptual states have accuracy conditions but not truth conditions. This, they hold, suffices for perceptual states to possess a kind of content that represents the world as being a certain way. To accept this is to accept that there is a kind of content that is subject to norms other than those having to do with truth and falsity. Result: Perceptual experiences are not intrinsically true or false. They have a kind of content that is more primitive than the content that propositional attitudes have.

The good news is that the notion of content in play for maximally minimal intellectualists is less demanding. Hence, the prospects of explaining such perceptual content by some means are better than they would be were it assumed that perceptual content is truth conditional. Or so it might seem. We will revisit this issue at the start of the next chapter.

The bad news is that this development has an important explanatory disadvantage. For the one major virtue of thinking of perceptions as propositional attitudes is that it makes it easy to see how they might intelligibly interface, in virtue of their contents, with other states of mind. Addressing the "intelligible interface" problem is more fundamental than and logically distinct from addressing the more frequently discussed issue of how it might be possible for perception to stand in epistemic relations, such as justification, with attitudes such as beliefs.

Perceiving that P is not judging, or believing, that P. However, it is at least possible to understand how these attitudes connect in virtue of their contents if "in perception you 'entertain' a judgeable content" (Noë 2004, p. 189). If the content of perception were propositional, then at least there would be no logical difficulty in conceiving that "I need only import the content of my perceptual state into cognition to believe it" (Heck 2007, p. 117).

In a nutshell, adopting new-style nonconceptualism about perceptual content appears to be inevitable for anyone who is persuaded that perceptual content is essentially nonconceptual. But making this move undercuts the most powerful philosophical motivation for believing that perception must be contentful: its power to address the "intelligible interface" problem.

Thus, whereas there was a clear motivation for believing that perception might have propositional content of the sort modeled on that which can be linguistically expressed, it isn't clear why we should believe in perceptual content of the restyled nonconceptual kind. At least, there is no gain in positing such contents when it comes to dealing with the "intelligible interface" problem.

Perception is unlike belief in another way too. As we noted earlier, minimal intellectualists reject that perception is modular—at least if modules are defined in Fodor fashion. Still, they must accommodate the fact that perceptual attitudes are independent and autonomous from higher and more central cognitive processes based on propositional attitudes such as belief. Our susceptibility to visual illusions, for example, has taught us that if there are perceptual contents they do not get revised and updated in the light of new evidence in the way that beliefs do.

Happily, it is possible to hold on to the idea that perception is isolated from central and open-ended inferential processes without assuming that perception is modular. One might, for example, hold that perceptual attitudes are special sorts of contentful attitudes—attitudes that are unlike beliefs in the critical respect that they are not revisable in the light of evidence. Perceptual attitudes, as a class, appear to fit the profile of what Tamar Gendler (2008, p. 557) calls *aliefs*:

To have an alief is, to a reasonable approximation, to have an innate or habitual propensity to respond to an apparent stimulus in a particular way. It is to be in a mental state that is . . . associative, automatic and arational. As a class, aliefs are states that we share with non-human animals; they are developmentally and conceptually antecedent to other cognitive attitudes that the creature may go on to develop. Typically, they are also affect-laden and action-generating.

Aliefs are unlike belief in just the way required. They have a different functional profile and a different job description: "[B]elief aims to 'track truth' in the sense that belief is subject to immediate revision in the face of changes in our all-things-considered evidence" (ibid., p. 565). Aliefs decidedly lack this feature—they are not revisable in the light of the individual's other contentful attitudes or beliefs.

Despite being importantly different from beliefs and other propositional attitudes, aliefs are nevertheless conceived of as representational states of mind having some sort of content. Paradigmatic aliefs, we are told, have content that is representational, affective, and behavioral. Thus, Gendler tells us that the BB-chasing behavior of a frog "can be explained by an alief with the content that might be expressed, among other ways, as follows: The frog alieves (all at once, in a single alief): small round black object up ahead; appealing in foody sort of way; move tongue in its direction" (ibid., p. 559).

Maximally minimal intellectualism not only abandons the commitments of hyperintellectualism; it regards perceptions as nonconceptual contentful attitudes—attitudes that have importantly different kinds of content and very different functional profiles than propositional attitudes such as beliefs. This lessens its explanatory burdens considerably and has the potential to avoid the problems associated with deflationary approaches to content. Therefore, maximally minimal intellectualism is REC's most interesting CIC rival.

6   CIC's Last Stand

The task is . . . not so much to see what no one has yet seen; but to think what nobody has yet thought, about that which everybody sees.
—Erwin Schrödinger

Once More unto the Breach

While unquestionably CIC-ish, maximally minimal intellectualism occupies a position that closely neighbors REC in conceptual space. There is much the two agree on. They remain rivals, logically excluding one another, because the former conceives of perceptual experience as essentially representationally contentful. This is the sticking point.

Maximally minimal intellectualism is the most modest, the least expensive, and, to our minds, the most plausible CIC proposal. It would convert into REC if it only abandoned the idea that perception possesses content that is essentially nonconceptual, trading that thought for the idea that perceiving is contentless. It's the position to beat. For this reason, examination of its chances of successfully motivating a need for and delivering on the promise of a theory of perceptual content provides the ideal means of framing and focusing on the pivotal questions: Are there any compelling grounds for thinking that perceiving is essentially representational? If so, what are they? In what follows, we consider the most promising current strategies for addressing these questions and find them wanting. We conclude that there is, as yet, nothing on offer from the friends of CIC that should persuade us that perceiving cannot be, and in fact is not, contentless.

Operation Imagistic Cognition

Gauker (2011) fiercely defends the premise that all conceptually based thought and judgment depends on language. Yet he also insists that there exists a powerful nonverbal, and hence nonconceptual, similarity-based mode of thinking and experiencing—a form of imagistic cognition. At its heart, this capacity, common to humans and many other animals, is guided by nothing more than a capacity to appreciate the similarities that hold between things.

Gauker asserts that the existence of this type of cognition explains how nonverbal perceivers are able to perform many sophisticated tasks, including tracking objects, navigating through space and time, and analyzing imagistic cause-effect relations. (See chapter 5 of Gauker 2011. For similar claims, see chapter 4 of Hutto 2008.) All this is possible, Gauker claims, without it being the case that perceivers must classify or categorize what they are dealing with by thinking that the objects in question belong to a particular kind (2011, p. 185). As he tidily summarizes, "*Of course*, animals think! . . . Nothing follows about whether they think *conceptually*." (ibid., p. 163)

So far, this is all completely in step with and acceptable to REC. However, Gauker goes further and claims that this kind of cognition is essentially representational, despite being thoroughly nonconceptual:

[T]here is a kind of cognition that *employs representations* that are not conceptual but which are more than a mere impetus to thought, because they themselves are medium to a kind of problem-solving. It can guide behavior without the intervention of conceptual thought at all. (2011, p. 145, emphasis added)

How is this so? Making use of the standard machinery of correspondence (machinery familiar from traditional theories of truth and content), Gauker imagines that an internal, brain-bound perceptual similarity space exists and that it "maps into" an objective quality space (ibid.).[1] He maintains that objects of perception have gradable qualities—not only familiar qualities (size, shape, color, and so on) but also qualities of a kind that come less readily to mind, such as jerkiness of motion. From this platform Gauker advances the view that an object's location in objective quality space is fixed by the way it is situated in a wide range of dimensions of perceptible variation. Representation of items in the objective quality space is possible, Gauker claims, because each mind/brain contains a perceptual similarity space that systematically relates to it. The perceptual similarity space "maps into" (which looks very like what in more traditional lingo one would call "mirroring") the corresponding dimensions of objective quality space.

On this view, when an object or a scenario is perceived perfectly accurately a mark is placed in the perceiver's perceptual similarity space such that it precisely records the object's or scenario's location in objective quality space. This sort of mark, if it is caused in the right way, constitutes an accurate perceptual representation. Misperception occurs when a mark is recorded in perceptual similarity space that fails to correspond to the actual location that the object occupies in objective quality space. In this way, allegedly, perception can be inaccurate or non-veridical, even in the absence of conceptually based judgments. (For details, see p. 198 of Gauker 2011.)

What determines whether a token marking is right or wrong? Gauker's basic answer to this question relies on the idea that there is a "functionally normal way in which perceptual similarity space guides behavior" (2011, p. 196). It is by appealing to this notion that Gauker hopes to account for the difference between accurate perceiving and mere misperceiving. He appeals to norms set by biology. Hence, for him the norms of perceptual accuracy and inaccuracy are fixed by facts of natural history.

This commitment is indelibly clear when we consider Gauker's two definitions of the normal function of perceptual similarity space. His first approximation speaks only of a way of guiding behavior that evolutionary pressures will have directly selected for. But his second formulation is expanded to include the possibility of learning, such that the normal function in question denotes "a way of guiding behavior that accounts for the promulgation throughout the species through a process of natural selection of a function from learning histories to perceptual similarity spaces" (2011, p. 197).[2]

Gauker also recognizes that these ways of understanding what grounds accuracy have to be enhanced or supplemented if they are to provide a basis for making sense of persistent perceptual illusions. This is because making room for visual illusions in the natural order requires accommodating the possibility that there are inaccurate responses that, despite conforming to natural design, are in some other respect "sub-optimal" (ibid., p. 196). We will return to this thread in the next section, where it will prove polemically useful.

Here we wish only to highlight the problems that ensue from taking the first and most fundamental step: relying on biology to set the norms required for accuracy and explain the kind of content nonconceptual representations possess—the kind of content that is allegedly essential for perceiving.

Had Gauker proposed the above account as a basis for understanding representational content as traditionally conceived (i.e., as truth conditional), we would, at this point, simply use arguments presented in chapter 4 as grounds for dismissing it. Ultimately, our verdict is that this more modest proposal suffers from the exactly the same problems evinced in chapter 4. But in order to show resoundingly why this is so, we will have to iron out a slight wrinkle.

Standard teleosemantic theories of content are very clear that they aspire to provide a naturalized theory of mental representations on the assumption that representations possess truth-conditional content. Millikan (2005, p. 93) announces that "intentionality has to do with truth conditions." For her this is so across the board: "[T]he intentionality of language is exactly parallel to the intentionality of bee dances." (p. 98) Papineau's ambition is, likewise, to provide a "naturalistically acceptable explanation of representation: namely that the biological purpose of beliefs was to occur in the presence of certain states of affairs, which states of affairs counted as their truth conditions" (1987, p. xvi). More crisply, McGinn writes that the aim is to say how "teleology turns into truth conditions" (1989, p. 148).

We argued in chapter 4 that such theories fail to deliver the promised goods. No one should doubt that creatures can respond to features of current environments in ways that are out of step with the ways that their ancestors would have responded when the kind of responses in question were originally selected for. No doubt responses that are the products of evolution can be misaligned in this limited sense. But this does not establish that in doing so the imagined creatures are "getting things wrong"—that they are representing features of the world in a way that violates a norm of truth. Fundamentally, as Stich aptly highlights, "natural selection does not care about truth; it cares about reproductive success" (1990, p. 62).

It might be thought that Gauker escapes these problems by switching from a commitment to naturalizing truth conditions to the lesser task of naturalizing accuracy conditions. In effect, his tactic is to lighten the explanatory load. But this simply doesn't work, since the norms required for explaining accuracy are not easier to explain by appealing to biological facts than norms of truth. Thus, in failing to make any advance on familiar failed theories of content discussed in chapter 4 (he explicitly relies on a Millikanesque theory of content), Gauker fails to provide enough to account for accuracy conditions. Making room for the possibility of accurate or inaccurate perception in the natural order—i.e., making room for the possibility of contentful perceiving in the natural order—requires something more than a simple appeal to the norms established by biological proper functions.

Replacing truth conditions (or their ilk) with accuracy conditions is not a significant enough adjustment. Though doing so obviates the need to have to explain the norms of truth naturalistically, the norms of accuracy—if they imply the existence of robust representational content—remain sufficiently difficult to accommodate, as they require more than can be provided by appealing to biological functionality. There is a fundamental mismatch between the kinds of norms associated with truth or accuracy and those associated only with biological functionality. To the extent that it invokes norms at all, biology entails norms of the wrong kind for doing the sort of work Gauker requires of them. Although natural signs guide (and misguide) an organism's end-direct responding, and although this can be assessed normatively in just the way that Gauker (following Millikan) proposes, there is no reason to think these facts suffice for such responses to have or carry content.

Don't take our word for it. At least one prominent defender of maximally minimal intellectualism admits that there is a serious problem with this sort of proposal, reaching precisely the same verdict that we do for the same reasons. Burge (2010, p. 301) acknowledges that there is "a *root* mismatch between representational error and failure of biological function." Two pages later, he uses a slogan that echoes Stich: "Evolution does not care about veridicality. It does not select for veridicality *per se*."[3] Gauker's strategy cannot hope to hold the line at perceptual experience for CIC. Operation Imagistic Cognition is a nonstarter. But perhaps there is another way to defend CIC's position on this front.

Operation Perceptual Science

Burge (2010) bids to do better. He agrees with our assessment that none of the aforementioned attempts to naturalize content succeed. He regards them as failed products of a deflationary tradition—one that, time and again, makes the mistake of trying to understand representation in inappropriately reduced terms. The continual error is to appeal to the wrong types of phenomena to make sense of representation and to focus on the wrong branches of science for inspiration. The result, as Burge sees it, is systematic overstretching, diluting, and indeed debasing of the notion of representation.

What does Burge offer in the place of this failed deflationary tradition? Not another reductive theory of content. Burge adopts a unique and subtler strategy for securing CIC's cause than what its other friends offer. Two features of it are worth highlighting.

First, Burge is uncompromising in his understanding of what is minimally required of mental states that have proper representational functions. The function of representational states—which includes all perceptual states—is essentially predicative. It is to pick out various purported particulars and to attribute various properties to them. Examples of attributed properties include "being cube-shaped," "being green," "being in certain directions," and "being at certain distances." The content of perceptual states is defined by such contentful attributions, which can be more or less accurate. Functioning in this way, representational contents come with built-in veridicality conditions. For Burge, the function of perception is to produce veridical representations—it succeeds when doing so, and this is, allegedly, a good for the perceptual system. However, in line with his ardent anti-reductionism, the "relevant notions of success and failure are not those of biological success and failure" (2010, p. 308). Veridical perceptual states succeed or fail in their own special way:

An individual's perception falls under representational norms for successful formation of perceptual states, given the individual's perceptual capacities. Natural norms apply even if an individual cannot understand or be guided by them.[4] (p. 314)

Second, and more crucially, Burge trades on the authority of perceptual science and common sense in making the general case that we have no choice but to believe that perceptual representations with content exist. He maintains that contentful representations are the primitive posits of perceptual science. That they exist is the fundamental, grounding assumption of the science. Assuming this to be so, Burge refuses to make the familiar mistake of trying to explain representation in more basic terms. He regards "contentful representation" as an irreducible yet scientifically well-established construct—one that has already more than earned its explanatory keep. In lieu of yet another (failed) reductive proposal about the basis of representational content, we are offered assurances that the credentials of this posit are in impeccable scientific order.

According to Burge, mental states with representational functions and features figure centrally as distinctively psychological explanantia and explananda in the perceptual sciences. The perceptual sciences are awash with "explanations that give perceptual and other representational states *a causal role* in engendering animal action, and in causing further psychological processes. Such explanations evince the existence of perceptual states" (2010, p. 310, emphasis added). And it is not just that perceptual science trades in and provides explanations involving representations. Part of its raison d'être is to explain representational phenomena. Thus,

Veridicality, fulfillment of representational function, is the central *explanandum* of visual psychology. Illusions are explained as lapses from normal representational operation, or as the product of special environmental conditions. Visual psychology explains visual perception. It explains seeing. Seeing is fundamentally veridical visual representation. (p. 311)

No substantial thesis about content is provided—nor, if Burge is right, is any required. Burge's approach is like that of Hill, who also provides a list of reasons for believing in the truth of CIC without attempting to provide "a general theory of the nature of representation" (2009, p. 257). For those electing to take this route, belief in CIC is neither motivated by nor dependent on the production of a theory of content. We can know CIC to be true because of the successes, the stability, and the empirical fruitfulness of sciences that deploy robust representations in their explanations and seem to explain essentially representational phenomena. According to Burge, this is undeniably true of the perceptual sciences, visual psychology marking out the clearest case. Successful perceptual science thus, at once, "assumes" and "vindicates" CIC. (See Burge 2010, pp. xiv and 88.)

If Burge is right, this eliminates the need for a reductive explanation of robust representational properties. No naturalized theory of content is needed. Representations are primitive posits of an autonomous science of perception whose theoretical bet has been thoroughly vindicated by its successes. This is Burge's basis for thinking that "we know *empirically* that there are perceptual states with such accuracy conditions" (2010, p. 310). We are to take it on good faith that vision is essentially representational, essentially attributive. By contrast, Burge insists that anti-representationalist approaches, such as REC, are "refuted by" and "incompatible with" mature, well-grounded perceptual science (ibid., pp. 23 and xvii). Strong words.

Without further augmentation, Burge's proposal is profoundly philosophically unsatisfying. Even if we assume that contentful states of mind must exist because they are required by perceptual science, this does nothing to address deeply puzzling questions about how this could be so. It is, in effect, to argue from the authority of science. We are asked to believe in representational content even though none of the mysteries surrounding it are dealt with—and perhaps none of them may ever be dealt with. For example, how do the special kinds of natural norms of which Burge speaks come into being? What is their source, and what is their basis? How can representational contents *qua* representational contents cause, or bring about, other mental or physical events?

Putting this concern aside, we agree with Burge about the minimal conditions for a contentful representation. Yet we disagree about the so-called fact that Burge cites in order to rally support for CIC. Put simply, our objection is that there is no empirically known truth that establishes a robust connection between the explanatory successes of the perceptual sciences and the existence of perceptual states with representational content. If we are right about this, the existence of perceptual representations is not, *pace* Burge, secured by the mere existence of successful perceptual sciences.

A good way to put these competing views to the test, at least at a first pass, is by giving close scrutiny to what scientists actually say about the visual capacities of some prominent members of the Anura family in the class Amphibia—frogs and toads. Focusing on these animals is an ideal choice for several reasons.

First and foremost, as Neander (2006, p. 169) convincingly argues, frogs and toads are not "toy examples." Neander's welcome and detailed reportage on the topic of their brain and behavior, intended to bring philosophers up to speed on the basic empirical facts, reveals that, although anurans' brains are simpler than those of many other vertebrate species (making them easier to study), they nevertheless share the same broad principles of operation. Of course, this does not suggest that the study of anuran brains is easy: "Five decades of intensive research further on, biologists are still trying to unravel the complexities." (ibid., p. 170)

Neander (2006) highlights the following useful facts: Neuro-ethology teaches us that anurans' retinal cells are more complex than those of mammals. There is compelling evidence that the perceptual capacities of such creatures depend on activity in a mid-brain structure (the optic tectum) and not only the retinal ganglia. Their behavioral response profiles show that they reliably differentiate, perceptually, three broad categories: prey, predators, and others. Nor, despite philosophical lore which has them slavishly chasing flies, are frogs "fussy eaters." "In their natural environment they eat a variety of insects, including sowbugs, spiders, damselflies, crickets, leafbugs, spittlebugs, and short-horned grasshoppers." (ibid., p. 170)

Of direct concern for our purposes, it is also clear that anurans' perceptual capacities cannot be adequately understood in terms of mere feature detection. Indeed, they cannot be understood as an aggregation of feature-detection responses (for example, a summation of responses to shape and to motion). Rather, "the response is provoked by what is called 'configural features' (or sometimes a 'gestalt'), here, motion relative to shape" (ibid., p. 174).

A second reason why focusing on anuran perception is a good choice is that Burge definitively places frogs (as well as fish and octopi) on the list of perceivers. All these creatures unquestionably make the cut as full-blooded (if cold-blooded) perceivers because they can perceive basic constancies (Burge 2010, p. 420). We agree on both counts. But Burge makes additional claims that we don't accept. For him, a capacity to perceive constancies suffices for objectification, which, in turn, entails the existence of attributions, and thus representational content.

Perceptual constancy as defined in the scientific literature occurs when an individual perceives stable properties of objects despite variable sensory stimulation. Perceptual constancy (of size, color, and shape) is exhibited if such distal properties are seen despite changes in proximal stimuli.

For Burge, the capacity to see constancies entails the existence of attributions, implying the existence of representational content with conditions of satisfaction. Accordingly, on his view, attribution and representation must be in place wherever there are perceptual systems that exhibit constancy. As he sees it, constancies imply "capacities to represent environmental attributes, or environmental particulars, as the same, despite radically different proximal stimulations" (2010, p. 114). This follows because, in Burge's view, perceiving perceptual constancies entails objectification, which he defines as the "formation of a state with a representational content that is as of a subject matter beyond idiosyncratic, proximal, or subjective features of the individual" (ibid., p. 397). To objectify is to perceive more than is provided by the stimulus, and thus to definitively move beyond forms of responding that are directly guided by mere sensory stimulation. Wherever perceptual constancies are found in nature, we are sure to find contentful perceiving. Assuming Burge's framework, the mere existence of perceptual constancies guarantees contentful attributions are in play.[5]

The most reliable indicator that any individual is an objectifying perceiver is that it exhibits a capacity to localize—i.e., to determine the direction and the distance—of a "distal source of stimulation *without serial sampling*" (Burge 2010, p. 427). Frogs are known to exhibit two types of such localizing behavior: they orient toward or away from interesting stimuli, and they target and snap at prey.[6] So anurans not only exhibit basic perceptual constancies; they also exhibit perceptual constancies plus localizing abilities.

Since we plan to undermine Operation Perceptual Science by putting Burge's claims in favor of CIC on trial, Neander proves the ideal (because hostile) witness for us to call. She openly supports the ideas that anurans perceptually represent and that they contentfully represent (2006, p. 169). Indeed, her ambition is to provide an empirically driven and respectably grounded rationale for the assignment of contents in advance of (and hence in the absence of) a developed and agreed-upon theory of representational content. Her ambition is to serve the needs of mainstream cognitive science.[7] Nevertheless, having looked closely at what the relevant scientists have to offer, she doesn't suppose that their working assumptions include a commitment to the idea the perceivers being studied are representing—certainly not in any obvious or robust way.

Looking, for example, at what neuroethologists say, Neander admits—despite her sympathies—that "the truth is that they rarely if ever utter sentences beginning with 'the content of a +T5(2) is . . .' or '+T5(2)s mean . . .', or '+T5(2)s represent. . . .'" (ibid., p. 183)[8] Indeed, she continues,

I have to concede to those who dislike talk of content in the case of such simple systems that there is little explicit talk of error concerning *what* is represented. However, there is no hesitation when it comes to talk of error with respect to the localization content in this or similar cases . . . and neuroethologists do talk about the toad trying to catch 'inappropriate stimuli'. For example, if after ablation of the thalamus the toad orients toward a large looming square or the experimenter's hand (remember a normal toad only orients toward prey-like stimuli) that might be described as a response to an 'inappropriate' stimulus. It is interesting that the normal toad's response is not spoken of as inappropriate (as far as I have seen). (ibid., p. 184)

The last point might be thought to lend Burge some succor, but Neander's use of scare quotes around 'inappropriate' is perhaps telling. It certainly demands that we tread with some caution. More important, Neander's further analysis of what perception scientists take object recognition to involve reveals that they are only committed to the idea that it boils down to "the recognition of a configuration of visible features (i.e. those related to size, shape and motion relative to shape of the stimulus)" (ibid., p. 183). This is quite plausible (especially in the light of the response profiles of the unimpaired animals in their natural settings), but it falls a good way short of what Burge needs in order to secure CIC. All we can safely surmise from the above exercise is that perception scientists are committed to something weaker than what Burge needs.

The perceptual sciences, it seems, would not collapse if it turned out that true perceivers fall into the class of aspectual respondents but not that of attributive claimants, as REC assumes. On such a view, perception doesn't depend on, or entail, the existence of attributive states of mind—states that attribute, say, X's being F. Rather, it depends on, and entails the existence of, aspectual states of mind according to which X looks or feels F.

As Tye (2009, p. 88) observes, the common assumption that perceptual experiences must be contentful is "most strongly motivated by the thought that, in seeing objects, [1] they look some way to us, [2] together *with the further thought* that an object can look a certain way only if it is experienced as being that way. This in turn, [3] *seems to require* that the object be represented as being that way." (emphases added)

The crux is that we accept [1] and [2] as well as the link between them, but deny that [2] implies what seems to be the case in [3]. It can't be assumed *a priori* that representational and attributive capacities are present whenever things look a certain way to perceivers.

Perhaps, at this juncture, it might be thought that scientists are not the people best placed to say what does the real work in their theorizing. Hence, their failure to use robust representational language might simply reflect the fact that they are not primarily concerned with and attuned to constitutive questions of the sort that interest philosophers. Perhaps they are confused or ignorant about the true explanatory basis of their sciences in the way theorists in other branches of science are confused or ignorant when they claim to posit robust representations when in reality (if Burge is correct) they only operate with a deflated and debased notion of representation at best. Though this might keep some hope alive for CIC, it hardly settles matters in its favor. Certainly there is no uncontroversial, simple, non-question-begging appeal to be made to already agreed-upon and established facts about what drives the successes of the perceptual sciences that could support either side in this debate.

Let us be clear about our strategy. We are not proposing to directly counter Burge's offensive by arguing that the truth of REC is secured by appealing to the authority of perceptual sciences. Rather, we are undermining the support that Burge thinks such sciences supply, unequivocally, to CIC.

We are happy to allow that exactly what such sciences do and don't assume is open to interpretation and further argument. For all we need to establish at this stage in order to queer the pitch for Burge's defense of CIC is to show that there are live questions about the extent to which the perceptual sciences *in fact* assume representational notions. Moreover, there would be live questions about the extent to which such assumptions are tied to explanatory successes of such sciences even if the perceptual sciences *did* assume representational notions. If it should turn out that, as we suspect, no such commitment exists, then

Burge's plan for rescuing CIC not only fails; it backfires. Even though the reasoning that leads up to his plan is boldly honest and welcome, his appeal to the successes of the perceptual sciences doesn't provide sufficient reason to believe in contentful representations with the properties Burge identifies. In a nutshell, it is far from obvious that the perceptual sciences assume (or need assume) the existence of contentful representations. It is even less obvious that their explanatory successes depend on doing so.

There is one outstanding issue. What about perceptual illusions? The very idea of such illusions seems to imply veridicality conditions. Surely to be subject to perceptual illusions is to be in violation of natural norms of the sort to which Burge alludes above—and that is possible only if there is perceptual attribution and content. By this train of reasoning, the mere existence of visual illusions implies the existence of perceptual representations with content that can be evaluated as veridical or not.

What makes us confident that there are perceptual illusions of the sort that entails the existence of perceptual content is that there seem to be cases in which the content of what we see conflicts with the content of what we know and what we ought to believe. The Müller-Lyer illusion (figure 6.1) is the paradigmatic example of such an illusion. We perceive the two parallel lines as being of two different lengths even after we are made aware of and come to believe the contrary—that they are of the same length.

Reflection on cases of this kind motivates surety that perceptual illusions—those that entail content—exist. But there is a serious problem for Operation Perceptual Science. Our certainty that the content of our perceptual attitude conflicts with the content of our informed belief requires us to ascribe a

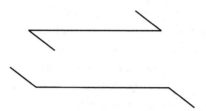

Figure 6.1
A version of the Müller-Lyer illusion

full-fledged, conceptually informed propositional content to our perceptual state. The two states of mind can come into conflict only if they each possess token contents that disagree in what they claim. But that can happen only if they are contents of the same general kind.

Obviously, this does not sit well with the fact that Maximally Minimal Intellectualism denies that perceptual attitudes have propositional contents. Let that pass. A more fundamental concern is that we can know with confidence that we are subject to perceptual illusions in this sort of case only if the Expressibility and Accessibility assumptions (as discussed in the preceding chapter) are honored. It must be the case that we can readily say, and hence readily know, what the content of our perceptual state is *without having to engage in any empirical investigation.* For example, it is only because we allegedly know that our perceptual state attributes "length" that we are certain we are subject to an illusion when confronted with the Müller-Lyer arrows. The *only* evidence that there is an illusion here is the conflict between the content of our perception and the content of our better-informed belief.

But if that is right then it looks as if perceptual illusions (those of the sort that entail content) depend for their very existence on high-level interpretative capacities being in play. The former are parasitic on the latter. Accepting this, like Gauker (2011), we take it that when it comes to perceptual illusions our capacity for propositional judgment has a kind of analytical priority. Consequently, there is "a distinction between accurate and inaccurate perceptions only for creatures that are capable not only of perception but also of conceptual judgment" (Gauker 2011, p. 205). It follows that "we are in no position to attribute illusory perceptions, similar to our perceptions of the Müller-Lyer arrows, to a creature that lacks the capacity for judgment" (p. 205). The crux is that if a creature is incapable of making judgments then it cannot be regarded as subject to persistent illusions. Certainly we have no evidence associated with the paradigmatic perceptual illusions of the sort to which we are subject for saying otherwise.

It might be thought that Operation Perceptual Science ought to attempt to tackle this problem, cleanly, from a different direction. Might it not invoke a tactic of austerely shunning any commitment to the Expressibility and Accessibility assumptions, sticking solely with the natural standards and norms that are discovered by the perceptual sciences themselves? After all, the trouble-making assumptions are sourced from our everyday, linguistically grounded practices for ascribing content—doubtless that is where the rot crept in.

This bold view has the consequence that it could turn out that most, if not all, of what we take to be canonical perceptual illusions are nothing of the sort. That would depend entirely on what our perceptual states are attributing in such cases. For example, perceptual science might discover that when confronted with the Müller-Lyer arrows our perceptual states are not attributing "length." One might be willing to bite the bullet on this. But the real trouble with this suggestion is that it is no longer obvious that there are any perceptual illusions of the required content-entailing sort. Thus, for example,

It is hard to think of any experimental manipulations that would show that, for example, a beaver was subject to the Müller-Lyer illusion. We might find that under certain circumstances, a beaver was reliably disposed to behave toward two logs of equal length as if it perceived one of them to be longer than the other. (Gauker 2012)

We can account for this sort of case by appealing to how things look to the beaver without assuming that something's looking a certain way entails that perceptions or experiences make attributions. This weaker way of understanding what is required for perceiving is consistent with the possibility that if things look somehow abnormal to an individual then we can expect that individual to respond in inappropriate ways to certain stimuli. But there is no compelling reason to suppose that inappropriate responding of such kind involves errors of content attribution.

The Phenomenal Cavalry?

Perhaps all is not lost for CIC yet. If we accept, as we do, that perceptual experience is aspectual—that things look or feel a certain way to perceivers—might this suffice to secure representationalism, albeit by a quite different path? Chalmers (2010, p. 371) holds, for example, that intentionality and phenomenality are "intimately connected"—that they are "intertwined all the way down to the ground." If that is so, satisfactory accounts of these phenomena—the most important phenomena of mind—must always speak to one another. With this in mind, Chalmers proposes an unusual sort of representationalism, advocating a nonreductive version of the claim that phenomenal properties entail representational content. Like Burge, he bucks the trend and rejects the deflationary tradition, allying himself more closely with those who believe that at least some important kinds of representational properties might be grounded in phenomenal properties (which also cannot be explained reductively).

Chalmers is of the view that experiences, insofar as they exhibit (and simply by exhibiting) phenomenality, automatically represent the world as being a certain way—a way that implies accuracy conditions. For him, phenomenality entails a specific kind of representational content with built-in conditions of satisfaction. Chalmers assures us that "it seems intuitively clear that perceptual phenomenology, by its very nature, involves representation of the external world" (2010, p. 344). Put more cautiously, his intuition is that it is "not implausible that there is something about consciousness that by its very nature yields representation of the world" (p. 371). He admits that this is a "substantive thesis" (p. 383), but he thinks there is good reason to accept it.

Just getting clear about the basic contours of Chalmers' thesis is a complex business. To give a full and detailed account of his views on this topic would require a substantial digression. Thankfully, that is not necessary in order to identify its Achilles' heel. For our purposes, a bare sketch suffices. Here it is: Chalmers defends the view that phenomenal representational content is a kind of Fregean content—a mode of presentation with a content that is captured by something like the following condition of satisfaction: the object or property that normally causes experiences of such and such a phenomenal type.

Despite assuming that the representational content of phenomenal experiences is Fregean, Chalmers acknowledges that Fregean content, as he defines it, lacks phenomenological adequacy. Moreover, it threatens to overintellectualize the phenomenal aspects of experience (a concern that lingers even if he can defend the idea that there are nonconceptual representational contents, as is his wont—see Chalmers 2010, pp. 368–369). To deal with this failing, he posits yet another kind of content—a much more peculiar kind: Edenic content.[9] Edenic content is introduced in order to help refine and supplement Chalmers' proposed account of the Fregean, representational content of experience. Edenic content attributes properties to the world on the basis of how things appear to us phenomenologically—such contents specify which properties would have to be instantiated if our experiences were to be perfectly veridical. But since we don't live in Eden, it turns out that there is a gap between how things seem to us and how they are. To use Chalmers' own example, we can, and often do, experience perfect redness even though our world, at best, instantiates only imperfect redness (where the latter might be some physical property, such as surface spectral reflectance).

Does this mean that the phenomenal Edenic content of perceptual experience always and systematically misrepresents? Chalmers denies this. Invoking a technical notion, he holds that imperfect redness "matches" perfect redness if it plays the role that perfect redness would have played in Eden—i.e., that of bringing about phenomenally red experiences. With this notion of matching in play, Chalmers aims to secure the idea that our representations are often veridical in an ordinary, imperfect sense. We can accept this, he thinks, as long as we are not overly demanding about what veridicality requires—that is, if we require less of it than would have been required of it in Eden.

Chalmers' final move is to suppose that phenomenal content has Fregean conditions of satisfaction that can be formulated in a revised way—with indispensable if tacit reference to Edenic content—in order to specify what phenomenal contents represent. He tells us, for example, that "a phenomenally red experience will be imperfectly veridical iff its object has the property that normally causes phenomenally red experiences" (2010, p. 403). Cast in this way, representational content is plausibly often satisfied, even in our imperfect, fallen world. Thus, "our experience *presents* an Edenic world and thereby *represents* an ordinary world" (ibid., p. 406, emphases added). Since the representational Fregean content of experiences is in this way parasitic on Edenic content, it turns out that "Edenic content is that key" (p. 454).

The trouble is that we are given no account of the origins and the basis of Edenic content. Chalmers offers no such explanation, nor does he pretend to. This is revealed, for example, when he asks, rhetorically, how mental states come by Edenic content, a notion that is pivotally important in his account. Disappointingly, but tellingly, he declines to answer, noting only that "we do not yet have a good theory of how mental states represent properties at all" (p. 418). That is surely true. Though this is wholly in line with his self-avowed non-reductionism, in the end the lack of explanatory power makes this sort of account questionable and unattractive.

But not only does this make Chalmers' account unsatisfying; it makes it rather incredible. The fact is that Chalmers offers no explanation that would help us to understand *how* experiential states of mind could possibly make inherent contentful demands on the world. In the absence of such an account, Chalmers' proposal faces a serious motivation problem. Far from being "intuitively clear" that simply having a certain qualitative experience—say, the redness of red—suffices to represent the world as being a certain way, it is not at all obvious that this is so, nor—indeed—how it could be so. Thus, a more robust account than Chalmers offers is required if, in lieu of its being made intelligible how phenomenality might entail robustly contentful properties, we might be persuaded to accept this thesis.

Nothing, other than an insight into Chalmers' intuitions, is provided to convince us that qualitative experiences, by themselves, attribute certain properties to reality—attributions that might be accurate or veridical. Yet, like Burge, in the absence of some more compelling considerations, we take it that "phenomenal consciousness is not in itself (that, just by virtue of being phenomenally consciousness) representational" (Burge 2010, p. 402). Appealing to the existence of phenomenal properties looks to be of no help to beleaguered CICers.

The Factual Cavalry?

Might there not be some other source of support for CIC? Might not perceptual experiences have representational content in a way quite different from those considered so far? After all, as Jackson and Pettit (1993, p. 269) remind us, "'content' is a recently prominent term of art and may well mean different things to different practitioners of the art."

One remaining possibility that we haven't yet considered in any detail is that perceptual contents might be Russellian propositions. Russellian propositions are structured entities with which we can be intellectually acquainted. In modern parlance, they are often identified with facts or obtaining states of affairs because they are structures composed of individuals, properties, and relations. Nevertheless, this easy assimilation overlooks special properties of components of Russellian propositions and the complexes themselves. Although Russell thought of them as forming the ultimate bedrock of the world, he also conceived of them as—essentially—potential objects of thought. He imagined them to be not only facts but also, at once, propositional contents. Accordingly, "true mental content is identical with worldly facts; it does not correspond to them . . . the content of the thought *is* the worldly fact" (Rowlands 2006, p. 24).

Yet, as Stalnaker helpfully reminds us, "it is essential to propositional contents that they have truth conditions" (1998, p. 341). Given this, how might something be both a fact—an obtaining state of affairs—*and* a proposition at the same time? Well, "one might . . . identify the content with the truth conditions themselves" (p. 343). On this view, what makes a certain thought true is the very object of thought itself. Interestingly in view of our arguments concerning the Hard Problem of Content in chapter 4, Stalnaker draws the very same connection that we highlighted: that some renderings of the notion of informational content are committed to understanding the former as Russellian propositional contents. Stalnaker helpfully makes the connection explicit by using "the label 'informational content' for content as truth conditions" (p. 343).

The idea that perceptual contents might be Russellian contents has had some prominent supporters in recent times. Speaks (2005) notes that this identification is at the heart of the influential view of content articulated in McDowell's *Mind and World*. Thus, Speaks finds it "natural to identify [early McDowellian] contents with Russellian propositions" (p. 376).

The very idea of Russellian propositions generates serious philosophical problems. (See chapter 1 of Hutto 2003/2006.) In chapter 4 we mentioned the tension between a metaphysics that regards propositional contents as making up, or constituting primitive parts of, the world and explanatory naturalism. We are persuaded by William James' (1909) views on these matters. Long ago, James exposed the fundamental confusion in Russell's thinking. James argued that the mistake is to conflate facts, or realities, with truths. On Russell's view, great swaths of the world are literally composed of "as yet unthought" contents. If, by contrast, we follow James' lead, we can, without such metaphysical extravagance, swap a commitment to the existence of such contents for talk of virtual truths—that is, of truths that could and would be expressed if someone were to express them. Accordingly, truth conditions come into being only when there are creatures that actually form propositional attitudes about some state of affairs. Hence, "if there is to be truth . . . both realities and beliefs about them must conspire to make it" (James 1909, p. 197). Strictly speaking, the existence of truth conditions, according to James, depends on the formation of contentful beliefs about worldly states of affairs. This is because "realities are not *true*, they *are*: and beliefs are true *of* them" (p. 196). James puts philosophical confusion on this score down to what he describes as the 'vulgar' tendency to confuse 'truths' with 'facts' (pp. 78, 144, 223). We agree.

At any rate, Russellians will have to provide some fairly compelling reasons if they are to make a convincing argument for thinking that facts logically entail contents. Surely we are not compelled to accept this *a priori*. If anything, *prima facie*, things seem to be as Bermúdez describes them:

Propositions are very different from states of affairs. In particular, propositions are true or false, while states of affairs are not the sort of things that can be either true or false. On many standard ways of thinking about propositions and states of affairs, states of affairs are the things that make propositions true or false. (2011, p. 404)

Is there any other weaker possibility for making sense of contents that we have overlooked? The new McDowell (2009) apparently thinks so. He advances a special version of the idea that human perceptual experience is contentful. For him, experience must be contentful because conceptual, representational thought can be applied to it. It is necessarily contentful because it is amenable to conceptualization. Our perceptual experience, McDowell thinks, must be conceptually shaped (2007a, p. 366). This is what makes it possible for us to bring our concepts to bear on it. Moved by this line of thought, McDowell claims that that "the content of an experience has [a distinctive sort of] form is part of what it is for the experience to be world-disclosing, categorically unified, apperceptive" (2007b, p. 348), and elsewhere on the same page that "when experience is world-disclosing, its content has a distinctive form." This is in line with McDowell 2009, where he tells us that "experiencing is not taking things to be so. In bringing our surroundings into view, experiences entitle us to take things to be so; whether we do is a further question" (p. 269). If we replace the talk of entitlement with talk of enabling, RECers can agree with this remark. However, we balk at the claim that these new considerations justify thinking that experience possesses a kind of yet-to-be-conceptualized content.

Although we accept that the notion of content has some leeway, it is wholly unclear what, for the new McDowell, motivates and justifies continued talk of content. It is not clear how to make sense of this new content qua content, since none of the standard notions (attribution, truth conditions, accuracy conditions) apply to it inherently. In the absence of any replacement notions that might do the required work, we recommend going all the way and ridding ourselves of the idea that perception is necessarily contentful. Having reached the very bottom rung on the ladder, it is not clear what "possessing content" really amounts to, or what work it is meant to do that couldn't be done just as easily by assuming that human beings share basic and content-free ways of responding directly to certain worldly solicitations and offerings.

Aftermath

Things can look or feel some way to individuals. That things look and feel a certain way does not entail that perceptual states possess or attribute content. Perceiving is, in and of itself, content-less—it lacks inherent conditions of satisfaction. There is simply no question of perceptual experiences', in and of themselves, being true or false, accurate or inaccurate, veridical or non-veridical. To suppose otherwise is to fall victim to overextending our everyday folk-psychological schema—applying notions where we shouldn't and assuming the existence of properties of mind where they don't belong.

7 Extensive Minds

The statement 'the mind is its own place', as theorists might construe it, is not true, for the mind is not even a metaphorical 'place'. On the contrary, the chessboard, the platform, the scholar's desk, the judge's bench, the lorry-driver's seat, the studio and the football field are among its places.

—Gilbert Ryle

From Extended to Extensive

What follows for the Extended Mind Hypothesis (EMH) if REC is true? The EMH was first formulated by Clark and Chalmers (1998) after being anticipated by others (Wilson 1994; Haugeland 1998). The big idea of the EMH is that external features of the environment—props, devices, or structures, such as sentences in notebooks—can become partly constitutive of the mental (Clark and Chalmers 1998, p. 12).

Nearly all discussions of EMH to date have proved unproductive, typically ending in stalemate. This is because those involved in these debates have not satisfactorily addressed the root issue. Their focus has typically been on special cases in which internal cognitive activity is augmented by certain external resources. Do these hybrids result in extended cognitive processes or systems in which the external resources become partly constitutive of mind? Parties on either side of the issue do not question that cognition should be understood in terms of the processing of representational or informational content.[1] They either tacitly assume or are openly wedded to CIC—indeed, they are committed to unrestricted CIC as long as they hold that *any and all* cognition must involve content in some way. By fully breaking faith with unrestricted CIC—kicking this CIC habit—REC enables the EMH debate to move ahead.

We can see the pivotal importance of CIC thinking for the way this debate is normally conducted by observing that the strongest objection to EMH takes the form of accusing its advocates of committing a causal/constitutive fallacy. All parties in this debate agree that external, environmental interactions matter for enabling and shaping cognition in nontrivial ways. But the critics of EMH insist that exogenous influences make nothing but purely causal contributions (see, e.g., Adams and Aizawa 2001, 2008, 2010; Fodor 2009)—that at best they play a merely supportive role in shaping and enabling cognition. In line with the Neural Assumption, discussed in chapter 3, critics of EMH take it that specific kinds of brain activities are necessary and sufficient for constituting mentality. Brain activity of the right sort is, for them, metaphysically sufficient for mind and cognition, even if it is not causally sufficient. This assumes that there is a sharp and principled division between what is truly constitutive of mind and cognition and what is merely causally necessary for mentality. Articulating where that divide falls requires specifying a criterion that separates the cognitive wheat from merely bodily and environmental chaff. The need for CIC kicks in when such a criterion of cognition (or a mark of the mental) is called upon by some internalist critics of EMH. Appeals are made to non-derived, original mental content, conceived of as informational or representational content of some sort.

Yet if the arguments of chapters 4 and 6 go through, it turns out that there are excellent reasons to be skeptical of any and all of these moves. If REC is right, basic cognition is not contentful; basic minds are fundamentally, constitutively already world-involving. They are, as we say, extensive. For to accept REC's thoroughgoing rejection of content in this domain is to reject the idea that basic minds might be non-extensive—i.e., essentially internal and brain-bound because contentful. In light of arguments of previous chapters, this simply cannot be the default option.

To suppose that what is constitutive of mentality must reside in organisms or their brains alone is to endorse a Senior Partner Principle holding that, although a partnership with environmental factors may be causally necessary for cognition, the organism's or system's brain "wears the trousers" in the relationship; only brains bring mentality to the party. In the place of this, we promote the more even-handed Equal Partner Principle as the right way to understand basic mental activity. Accordingly, contributions of the brain are not prioritized over those of the environment. (See also Hurley 2010.)

In this light, REC conceives of the mind as extensive, not merely as sometimes extended. It rejects what we dub the Default Internal Mind assumption (DIM). According to the Default Internal Mind assumption, basic minds are fundamentally brain-bound and—at best, if certain versions of EMH are true—are extended only in exceptional cases, such as when nonbodily add-ons are required to make the achievement of certain cognitive tasks possible. The Default Internal Mind assumption takes it for granted that, in their basic state, minds are unextended and brain-bound. If that is the case, then they become extended only when external resources are needed to complete certain cognitive tasks. On that model, what is fundamentally internal occasionally becomes extended.

By starting in the opposite place, REC alone provides the decisive means for silencing internalist critics of EMH. Indeed, accepting REC and rejecting the Default Internal Mind assumption inverts standard EMH thinking. Basic minds are fundamentally extensive, whereas special kinds of scaffolded practices must be mastered before anything resembling internalized, CIC-ish mentality appears on the scene. Success in some cognitive activities may depend on the exercise of highly structured, conceptually based competencies—competencies that may require the complex manipulation of vehicles with representational content.

REC assumes that acquiring capacities for engaging in such sophisticated CIC is possible only with the help of environmental scaffolding. Hence, it assumes that such capacities neither stem from nor have a wholly internal, neural basis. Rather, in line with a particular rendering of Sterelny's (2010) Scaffolded Mind Hypothesis, which is distinct from EMH in important ways, REC assumes that some "human cognitive capacities both depend on and have been transformed by environmental resources" (Sterelny 2010, p. 472).

Although we do not endorse EMH, we highlight the value of taking the REC line, which entails that basic minds are extensive, by examining the shortcomings of two main ways of motivating EMH: by appealing to parity and by appealing to complementarity. Both of these strategies, in different ways, give the internalists too much room for maneuver. As a result, they are systematically unconvincing to the opponents of EMH. Since neither side in the EMH debate offers anything decisive that could shift the opposition, the debate stagnates. According to our diagnosis, the fundamental problem with the standard strategies for motivating EMH is that they are simply not radical enough. Yet when they are radicalized, it is clear why we must trade in the notion of extended mind for that of extensive minds.

Parity-Motivated EMH

As originally advanced by Clark and Chalmers (1998), EMH said that—at least sometimes, when special conditions are met—features of the environment can co-constitute the mind. Clark and Chalmers illustrated this by focusing on the case of belief, using a thought experiment in which a slightly amnesic fellow named Otto uses a notebook to supplant his memory. Whenever Otto encounters something that he suspects may be relevant later but is likely to be forgotten, he writes it down in the notebook. Otto is imagined to be in New York and to have a desire to visit the Museum of Modern Art. Instead of digging up the address from his biological memory, he browses through his notebook, finds the address there, and heads off to 11 West 53rd Street. Clark and Chalmers (1998) argue that in this case Otto's *aide memoires* play roughly the same role that unconscious beliefs play for persons not affected by amnesia. They contrast Otto with Inga. When Inga wants to go to the Museum of Modern Art, she consults her biological memory, thereby activating her unconscious, lingering belief concerning the museum's location. If this suffices for regarding Inga's unconscious belief to be classed as mental, then, by parity of reasoning, we have every reason to adopt the same stance with respect to what is written in Otto's notebook. Clark and Chalmers' basic rule is that anything that plays the same functional role deserves the same cognitive status. Hence the Parity Principle:

If as we confront some task, a part of the world functions as a process which, were it done in the head, we would have no hesitation in recognizing as part of the cognitive process, then that part of the world is part of the cognitive process. (Clark and Chalmers 1998, p. 8)

The appeal to parity is utterly silent about the nature of mentality. It is advanced for strategic reasons to persuade those who are committed to internalism that there are no obvious grounds for rejecting EMH out of hand. Nevertheless, the neutrality of this strategy for motivating the EMH therefore does nothing, by itself, to undercut the Default Internal Mind assumption. As we shall show, it is precisely because of its quietism that this argumentative strategy allows internalists to dig in their heels, appealing to CIC thinking when insisting on their preferred criterion of the cognitive or the mark the mental. Internalists who assume the truth of some version of CIC have the perfect set of tools with which to accuse supporters of EMH of committing the causal/constitutive fallacy. Consequently, motivating EMH by appealing to parity alone does nothing to avoid this impasse—i.e., to block this familiar internalist move. Because this approach, on its own, has no means of moving the discussion along, it leads to stalemate.

Internalist critics of parity-motivated EMH (pEMH) claim that considerations such as those that Clark and Chalmers (1998) highlight can't establish anything more than that external features sometimes play supporting causal roles in enabling the completion of certain cognitive tasks. Without further backing, appeals to parity fail to show that the external features epitomized by Otto's reminders in his notebook ever truly co-constitute the mental.

A general CIC strategy is always available to internalists: If softer objections to EMH should fail, fall back on appeals to content of some kind in order to secure an argument based on the casual/constitutive distinction. We can see this, for example, in the way Adams and Aizawa (2001) argue against pEMH. They claim that parity doesn't hold—that external items never play the same roles as internal ones. They maintain that the chosen examples—external features allegedly co-constituting mental states, i.e., notes in a notebook playing the same role as biological memories—simply fail. This is because the external items in question aren't subject to the same psychological regularities that apply to whatever fulfills the relevant role internally. Otto's notes, for example, are not automatically updated or revised in the light of newly acquired information. By contrast, someone's biologically based belief about the location of the Museum of Modern Art will be automatically revised when she or he learns that all the buildings in New York City have been leveled by an exceptionally powerful earthquake (Weiskopf 2008).

Without further backing, this line of argument cannot succeed. Defenders of pEMH can justifiably point out that this internalist critique focuses only on contingent differences—differences that would disappear in the wake of appropriate technical developments. It is easy enough to imagine an electronic notebook being updated through wireless connections to the brain. What rules out the possibility that the processes deemed responsible for this updating in the brain might be functionally duplicated in an integrally environment-involving way?

When on the ropes, internalists play their ace. They reach for arguments that depend on what is allegedly a more principled difference between the external factors and the internal factors. Irrespective of the roles external features play, or the functions they fulfill, internalists argue that internal states—and *only* internal states—can bear, and be the source of, content. External items, it is said, lack content—and thus cognitive status—in and of themselves. They only acquire content and such status derivatively—*if* they are informed by mentality that is already contentful. Building on CIC, it is argued, in line with DIM, that mentality is—always and everywhere—internal, brain-bound.

One way to cash out this CIC commitment is to appeal to non-derived mental content. This idea has been knocking around for some time, but Adams and Aizawa claim that it is still in good shape and that none of the standard consider-ations—those emerging from work in robotics or from work on dynamical systems theory—"provide any compelling reason to doubt the existence of non-derived content, the viability of the derived/non-derived distinction, or the hypothesis that non-derived content is distinctive of cognition" (2008, p. 35).

Appeals to intrinsic or underived content, when not sup-ported by further theory, clearly fail to meet the needs of explan-atory naturalism.[2] This is most obvious in the case of Searle, who coined the term "intrinsic content." But the problem applies to any broadly Searley commitment to intrinsic content. To have a merely Searley commitment in this regard is to fail to meet the demands of a respectable cognitive science, one with appropri-ate explanatory ambitions.

Searle (1990) labors to show that computational paradigms of mind are hopeless. He rightly claims that proponents of such accounts try "to bully the reader into thinking that unless he accepts that the brain is some kind of computer, he is committed to some weird anti-scientific views" (p. 24).

Searle's favored alternative to computationalism is that "all of our mental life [is] caused by processes in the brain" (1984, p. 18). For him, brains are biological entities that are not essen-tially mechanical in nature. In a bid to distinguish his view from others in the field, he calls it "biological naturalism" and asserts that "mental events and processes are as much a part of our natural history as digestion, mitosis, meiosis or enzyme secretion" (1992, p. 1). For Searle, brains exhibit intrinsic consciousness and display original content because of peculiarities of their biological nature. Moreover, Searle holds that—lacking this nature, i.e., being inorganic—mechanical artifacts such as computers, no matter how sophisticated, can have no mental life.

Although Searle seeks scientific credibility for his account by allying himself with modern biology, his proposal is deeply unexplanatory and unilluminating. It is simply not good enough to be told that the intrinsic properties of consciousness and content have a biological basis. Naturalists want to know why, and precisely how, biological processes make mentality possible. That is an utterly reasonable demand in the light of Searle's own criticisms of standard cognitive science—i.e., his famous arguments designed to show that positing so-called symbols in a computational system does nothing to explain how such items can have representational properties. But, by the same token, how and why do biological brain states—just by being biological brain states—manage to exhibit consciousness and content? Searley biological naturalism lacks sufficient explanatory resources for providing answers to these questions. Bechtel (1988, p. 70) hits the nail on the head when he observes that Searle "must simply settle for asserting that intentional phenomena are biological and not attempt to explain how biology produces intentionality in the same manner as we can explain chemically how photosynthesis works. Intentionality, therefore, remains a mystery on Searle's analysis."

Adams and Aizawa explicitly do not follow Searle in rejecting computationalism. On the contrary, they write, "it is likely that,

as a matter of contingent fact, the kinds of computational processes we find operating over external representations, . . . will
turn out to differ from the kinds of *computational processes that we
find operating over representations in brains*" (2001, p. 59, emphasis added). Nevertheless, in sticking with an unexplained notion
of intrinsic content and making this the cornerstone of their
arguments against pEMH, Adams and Aizawa make no advance
on Searle's position. Only if they were to supply a naturalized
theory of content that justifies confining it to a cerebral locale
could their appeals to intrinsic content do the requisite non-
question-begging work. Ultimately, this would require either an
adequate response to the Hard Problem of Content described in
chapter 4 or the more modest alternative option for motivating
belief in content that we dismissed in chapter 6. In the absence
of such a response, relying on intrinsic content to undermine
pEMH is an empty gesture.

In light of those arguments, the same fate awaits *any* internalist appeals to CIC that are meant to provide a principled way of
defining cognitive status—even those that don't openly invoke
intrinsic content. For example, Adams and Aizawa (2010) claim
that it is possible to abandon a commitment to such content
without damaging their arguments. This move is credible only
as long as they can assume *some* notion of representation in
order to specify what is constitutive of the cognitive. "Suppose,"
they write, "we concede that there is no such thing as intrinsic
or non-derived representation. This, of course, leaves untouched
the idea that part of what distinguishes cognitive from non-
cognitive processes is the way in which cognitive processes
transform or manipulate mental representations." (p. 581)

Indeed, it is possible for someone defending this line to
go further still, appealing only to processes involving the

transformation or manipulation of purely non-representational, informational contents. That even weaker commitment would fit with Adams and Aizawa's hypothesis that "cognitive processing involves specific sorts of information processing not generally present in the familiar interactions humans have with tools in their environments" (2010, p. 581). But even this weaker move is blocked if the dilemma generated by the Hard Problem of Content discussed in chapter 4 is not satisfactorily dealt with.

The important thing to notice is that pEMH—on its own—lacks the resources to make any sort of conclusive reply to its internalist critics. Mere considerations of parity don't provide a decisive way of silencing EMH detractors. If the debate is to move along, a wholesale rejection of CIC in favor of REC is required in order to undermine any possibility of well-grounded support for the Default Internal Mind assumption.

Complementarity-Motivated EMH

It might be thought that there is another way to successfully motivate EMH without parity, and hence without the need to invoke REC. There have been attempts to motivate belief in EMH by appealing to considerations of integration or complementarity as opposed to parity (Menary 2007, 2010a, 2010b). Complementarity-motivated EMH (cEMH) has been described as a second wave in advancing the EMH cause (Sutton 2010).

We argue that cEMH has more to offer than pEMH, but only if its main insights are articulated in a context which assumes that contentless basic minds become contentful only when appropriately scaffolded. Without this adjustment to cEMH, we reach the same verdict about it that we reach about pEMH.

And so, by a different path, we come to the same conclusion: If the EMH debate is to be advanced, a more radical line must be followed.

If its advertising is to be believed, cEMH is better placed to deal with internalist critics than pEMH because it allegedly avoids buying into "the very position it is meant to displace" (Menary 2010a, p. 234). CEMH explicitly rejects pEMH because the latter tolerates DIM. Connectedly, cEMH criticizes pEMH for insisting that if external resources are to be cognitive then they should play a role that is identical, or similar, to the role—actual or counterfactual—played by internal cognitive resources. In this respect cEMH regards pEMH as too deferential.

In contrast, cEMH-ists propose that external features play an extending role, relevant to the mental, if manipulating such external features make acts and forms of cognition possible that would not be so by using internal means and resources alone. Thus the mind extends only in cases in which cognitive processes become a hybrid or amalgamated composite in which both internal and external features are necessary and in which internal and external features play different roles.

Nevertheless, unless they fully reject CIC-ish thinking about basic minds, proponents of cEMH fail in their ambitions to do better than pEMH in advancing the EMH cause. This is because cEMH is vulnerable to exactly the same internalist move that ultimately stalls the EMH debate when only pEMH is in play. Once again, it turns out that the only decisive way to clear the blockage is to take the stronger, REC line.

Specifically, cEMH gets into trouble too when it either fails to rule out or, worse, explicitly retains a CIC characterization of the internal resources that are thought to complement what is supplied by external features. For to do so allows internalists to help themselves to the CIC idea that basic minds are content involving in a way favorable to the Default Internal Mind assumption. Only by wholeheartedly rejecting CIC—a move that justifies a complete rejection of the Default Internal Mind assumption—can standard internalist responses to cEMH be completely and finally dispatched. But to call on REC for this sort of support ultimately requires shifting one's commitment from extended to extensive minds.

The central idea of cEMH is that genuinely hybrid, extended minds depend for their existence on external items' playing significantly different roles than internal ones (Sutton 2010). One might take this cEMH idea a step further, pressing that the mental is truly extended only if the combined integration of internal and external resources yields something that is cognitively new. (See Menary 2010a, p. 231.) This, of course, shifts the sense of extension. On this view, what matters is that novel cognitive capacities emerge, and that these capacities are made possible only by engagements with features of a wider environment.

This enhanced understanding of cEMH has roots in the work of Clark and Chalmers. For example, they regard the transformative power of language as a clear case of such cognitive augmentation:

Without language, we might be much more akin to discrete Cartesian 'inner' minds, in which high-level cognition relies largely on internal resources. But the advent of language has allowed us to spread this burden into the world. *Language, thus construed, is not a mirror of our inner states but a complement to them. It serves as a tool whose role is to extend cognition in ways that on-board devices cannot.* Indeed, it may be that the intellectual explosion in recent evolutionary time is due as much to this linguistically enabled extension of cognition as to any independent development in our inner cognitive resources. (1998, p. 18, emphasis added)

Menary (2007, 2010a) has developed this insight into a rich and nuanced position that provides a new framework for thinking about the EMH. He calls for a reconsideration of cognition in terms of enactive skills that can involve "bodily manipulations of external vehicles" (2010b, p. 229). He recognizes that such manipulations are normative, and that such norms—some of which will be socially grounded—determine "the content of environmental vehicles and how we manipulate them" (p. 229). He justifiably argues that if this is accepted then EMH must abandon the idea of "an internal cognitive system that is extended outward into the world" (p. 234). This comes very close to the view that it is possible to talk of contentful cognition only if there are externally grounded norms in play.

For all of this, taking the cEMH route provides no more protection against internalist objections than pEMH. This is because—on its own—cEMH allows CIC to remain in play. Hence, cEMH is entirely consistent with the existence of contentful internal vehicles, and internal manipulations thereof, even if extended minds come into existence only when these are coupled with external representational vehicles that do different work. The following quotation from Sutton expands on the differences between externally stored representations as opposed to biologically internal representations:

The storage and organization of information in Otto's notebook is . . . typically exogrammatic. Notably, information is stored there in discrete fashion, and representations in the notebook (linguistic or pictorial representations, for example) have no intrinsic dynamics or activity, are not intrinsically integrated with other stored information, and do no cognitive work in their standing or dispositional form. Representations in Inga's biological memory, in contrast, may well blend and interfere: according to connectionist accounts of memory, for example, non-occurrent standing representations, "stored" superpositionally in a single network's weight matrix, influence processing continually. . . . (2010, p. 197)

This quotation reveals that a commitment to CIC and the Default Internal Mind assumption is always a live option for cEMH-ists. Talk of the manipulation of internal vehicles that serve to complement the manipulation of external ones figures even in Menary's writings. "Cognitive integration," Menary notes, "benefits from the central insight of the extended mind hypothesis—some cognitive vehicles are bodily external, and manipulations of these vehicles are part of the overall cognitive process, which includes manipulations of *bodily internal vehicles*." (2007, pp. 58–59, emphasis added; see also Menary 2010, p. 238) Such remarks do no violence to cEMH, because all that is needed for the cEMH story is that complementary external and internal resources differ; no restriction is placed on the exact nature of such resources—for example, both might be content bearing, or only one or the other might be content bearing. It is thus open to cEMH-ists to accept CIC about basic minds, and some do. By itself, cEMH provides neither a rationale for nor any means of rejecting CIC. This is the crux.

It is consistent with cEMH that basic, biological resources may be contentful while external ones may lack content. With this option on the table, internalists can make precisely the same move that they make against pEMH. Internalists can insist that there is a difference between "merely causal" external resources and "truly constitutive" internal ones. For example, Adams and Aizawa fully accept the need for biologically basic forms of cognition to be augmented and extended by appealing to a wide range of external resources. But they in no way allow that this entails that such resources form any part of our minds—i.e., that the amalgamated system as a whole acquires cognitive status through such complementary coupling. All they admit is that "we are cognitively limited, and the use of non-cognitive tools helps us overcome these limitations" (2010, p. 588). Recognizing this problem, Wilson proposes a critical shift in thinking:

The shift is one from a focus on 'things', such as representations, to a concern with 'activities', such as the act of representing. Such activities are often bodily, and are often world-involving in their nature. A version of the problem of intentionality formulated so as to apply to them 'In virtue of what is activity A the representation of C?' seems hardly pressing at all. Rather, what cries out for discussion is the question of just what forms these activities take, and just how they bring about the effects they do. (2010, p. 183)

This consideration alone, however, cannot be used to defuse objections to the EMH based on the causal/constitutive fallacy. Focusing attention away from representational entities to representational activities doesn't help. How does this advance the case for cEMH? Internalists will surely be unmoved by this gambit, insisting that the relevant content-conferring representational activities are, as ever, brain-bound.

What Wilson has in mind is that the relevant activities are necessarily world involving—that they already incorporate external elements, such as chalk and a blackboard, pen and paper, a laptop computer, or a hand-held calculator—and that they do so essentially. Such environment-dependent acts of cognition—and nothing short of them—are meant to constitute "computing" or "solving a problem." But unsupplemented, this—of course—fails to address the real issue. Rather than providing an argument, this at best offers a "statement of extended cognition" (Adams and Aizawa 2010, p. 596).

Consider Wilson's example of calculating on a piece of paper. To an internalist, the environment-involving activity picked out in this example is cognitive only by grace of the presence of internal and intrinsically contentful activities, such as perception, interpretation, or planning. Only such internal and truly representational activities give the wider activity of writing its cognitive life. Therefore, in itself, focusing on activities rather than on "things" does nothing to undermine the internalist position. Only if Wilson's move is supplemented with a well-motivated rejection of CIC—of the sort that REC provides—is the dialectical situation transformed.

Partnering Basic Minds with Scaffolded Minds

In sum, without REC there is no way for defenders of EMH to motivate their position decisively and to silence internalist objections once and for all. However, invoking REC comes at a price. REC forces one to go beyond the EMH and to embrace the more radical view that basic minds are extensive and not just extended. To go with REC on the nature of basic minds is to go truly wide.

All of this follows if basic minds lack content. Yet if basic minds lack content then it is a mistake to talk of vehicles in this domain; the vehicle/content distinction has no purchase here. How then should we understand the limits and extent of basic minds if not in terms of content-bearing vehicles? We suggest, in line with a venerable tradition, that minds, quite generally, are best understood in terms of capacities.

As we have insisted from the outset, this is not to deny the existence and the importance of content and vehicles across the board. Contents and vehicles exist, but they are associated with linguistic symbols and forms of cognition that feature in and are logically and developmentally dependent upon shared, scaffolded practices.[3] This connects with the theme that cEMH is trying to promote, but that theme can be salvaged and advanced properly only under a REC banner, in an importantly different context.

Within a capacity-oriented framework it is possible to understand how basic minds are augmented through scaffolding in a different light. The capacity to think using contentful representations is an example of a late-developing, scaffolded, and socially supported achievement. It originates from and exists, in part, in virtue of social practices that make use of external public resources, such as pen, paper, signs, and symbols.

We can make sense of content-involving cognition by making reference to the cognitive gains brought on by individuals engaging in shared practices. The development of truly contentful thinking—as in performing arithmetic operations—depends on mastery of practices involving external symbols is fundamental. (For more on the transformative effects of this process, see chapter 5 of Hutto 2008; also see Menary 2007.) For example, a capacity for symbol-based calculating or reasoning, once it has emerged and has been learned, doesn't always and invariably occur by means of the manipulation of external elements. When an individual learns how to perform mental arithmetic, he or she does not do so by acquiring a capacity to manipulate bona fide internal symbols. Rather, what is gained is an ability to perform operations that previously required the manipulation of external symbols but have now become possible in the absence of external symbols.

Even when scaffolded cognition of this sort is performed offline, as is the case with mental arithmetic, it is not internal in any sense offensive to REC. Rather, it becomes (up to a certain degree) independent of context. Ironically, once this happens parity arises on the horizon again. For in such cases the capacity to engage in decoupled contentful activities is derived, in both a logical and a developmental sense, from activities that involve the manipulation of external vehicles. Scaffolded activities involving external symbols undoubtedly transform and augment cognition. This vindicates an insight of cEMH. However, the decoupled capacities that derive from such externally anchored cognitive augmentation are on a cognitive par with their external antecedents. The important point here is that the coupled activities are the ultimate basis of the decoupled ones, not the other way round—as the Default Internal Mind assumption would have it.[4]

Opting for the Scaffolded Mind Hypothesis over the Extended Mind Hypothesis also has the advantage of skirting the worry that the latter is of little use to psychological theorizing in general. This is because, at best, the EMH narrowly applies to the cognitive antics of lone individuals using highly trusted and entrenched external resources (Sterelny 2010, p. 476). In contrast, the Scaffolded Mind Hypothesis focuses on the communal and collective resources that stably augment and expand upon the resources provided by our basic cognitive capacities.

8   Regaining Consciousness

'What is a Caucus-Race?' said Alice; not that she much wanted to know, but the Dodo paused as if it thought that somebody ought to speak, and no one else seemed inclined to say anything.

'Why,' said the Dodo, 'the best way to explain it is to do it'. . . .

—Lewis Carroll, *Alice's Adventures in Wonderland*

Conflations of Consciousness

If basic minds are extensive because they are contentless, does it follow that phenomenality is likewise extensive? Headline-grabbing enactivist claims on this topic have attracted intense criticism, mixed with puzzlement. Enactivists assert that the phenomenal feel (or the what-it-is-like properties) of consciousness can be explained using their theoretical framework. The following sentence on page 960 of O'Regan and Noë 2001 exemplifies such assertions: "Our claim . . . is that it is confused to think of the qualitative character of experience in terms of the occurrence of something (whether in the mind or brain). Experience is something we do and its qualitative features are aspects of this activity." Augmenting this, Noë (2009, p. 9) claims that "my consciousness now—with all its particular quality for me now—depends not only on what is happening in my brain but also on my history and my current position in and interaction with the wider world." The assumption that phenomenality is determined by nothing short of specifiable interactions with environments can be read as the strong claim that phenomenality is literally constituted by such interactions, and hence that phenomenality is extensive, sprawling beyond the brain and into the environment.

Moreover, enactivists reject the idea that phenomenality implies the existence of qualia (understood as intrinsically qualitative, logically private, introspectable, incomparable, ineffable, incorrigible, atomic entities of our mental acquaintance). (See Dennett 1988, 1991.) Ultimately, this rejection leads enactivists to denounce the existence of an explanatory gap, effectively denying that there is a Hard Problem of Consciousness. For them, "qualia are an illusion, and the explanatory gap is no real gap at all" (O'Regan and Noë 2001, p. 960).

Critics of enactivism have understood neither what motivates and connects these claims nor what might justify them. In particular, they don't see how the strategy of going wide makes any advance on the Hard Problem of Consciousness. For them this move adds nothing. Prinz (2006, p. 17) sums up the concern:

Neuroscience is incomplete in one crucial respect: it can't explain why all these neural correlates feel the way they do. It can't even explain why they feel like anything at all. Perhaps this is the missing element that makes Noë feel like he has to go outside the head. If so, it's a fool's errand. For this deep epistemic problem of how physical states can be phenomenal experiences is in no way ameliorated by broadening the supervenience base. Just as it's hard to understand why brain states feel a certain way, it's hard to understand why brain states together with bits of the external environment would feel a certain way. As Noë realizes, wide supervenience will not help solve the hard problem of consciousness. So why go outside the head?

To understand what enactivism—and in particular REC—has to offer in this domain, we must disentangle how it intends to deal with the Hard Problem of Consciousness from claims about the extensiveness of phenomenality.

There is a way of bringing enactivist insights to bear on the Hard Problem of Consciousness (or Hard Problem, for short) to show that it isn't a real problem after all. Indeed, the Hard Problem is ultimately best avoided. For on close inspection the Hard Problem isn't just hard; it is impossible to solve (Hutto 2006; Cohen and Dennett 2011).

The standard picture of phenomenality assumes it is a unique mental phenomenon with the special properties listed above. As long as this picture remains in play, there can be no progress in understanding how phenomenality intelligibly relates to, or might be instantiated in, nature. The typical move, which is unilluminating and unconvincing, is to identify qualia with neural happenings of some sort while decrying the need to explain why such identities hold. We too endorse a strict identity thesis, but we accept that belief in such identities can and should be motivated. This is precisely where the enactivist strategy of rejecting the existence of qualia in conjunction with "going wide" shows its true worth.

But there's a twist. To understand phenomenality in a way that avoids the Hard Problem requires understanding it as part and parcel of world-involving sentient activity. However, doing so doesn't logically necessitate the view that phenomenality itself is extensive. Thus, it remains an open question whether the strategy of "going wide" for explanatory purposes implies that the minimal supervenience base for phenomenality is likewise wide (i.e., extensive). Although a full and satisfying understanding of phenomenality cannot be achieved without going wide, this fact is compatible with the supervenience base for phenomenality remaining entirely confined to the brain.

Going Wide While Staying In

Some enactivists argue that phenomenality has a wide supervenience basis—that it constitutively involves parts of the environment. We call their strongest arguments *Essential Involvement Arguments*. They assert that the brain processes that are necessary for phenomenality occur when, and only when, there is interaction with certain external circumstances. On this view, phenomenality requires not only the occurrence of certain brain processes but also certain extra-cranial conditions. Extra-cranial conditions form part of the minimal supervenience base of phenomenality. Phenomenal experience strongly supervenes on, or is constituted by, temporally extended, interactive worldly engagements. It is thus assumed that "experience is not caused by and realized in the brain, although it depends causally on the brain. Experience is realized in the active life of the skilful animal." (Noë 2004, p. 227)

Arguments against the possibility that phenomenality might supervene more narrowly come in varying degrees of complexity. Cosmelli and Thompson (2010) have tried to establish that the very idea of a brain-in-a-vat having phenomenal experiences is discredited because of the necessary presence of noncerebral metabolic processes (among many other conditions). Similarly, they and others have argued that persisting coherent visual phenomenology is impossible without the upkeep of actual interaction with a current environment (O'Regan and Noë 2001). This would explain why the analog of visual experience in dreams is less coherent.

As Hurley (1998, 2010) recognizes, cases in which the temporal dimension is predominant in making experience possible are most convincing when it comes to arguing for extensive phenomenality. (See also Clark 2009.) For this reason, when critiquing the wide supervenience view of experience, Clark focuses on special kinds of brain-body-environment interactions—those that involve Dynamical Entanglement plus Unique Temporal Signature, abbreviated DEUTS (2009, p. 980). He points to situations in which the relevant brain activity unfolds in a way that is uniquely dependent on precisely timed worldly interactions. Only by being led in the dance by the dynamic unfolding of a sequence of worldly events would this specific pattern of dynamic unfolding in the brain take place.

Clark (2009, p. 220) takes the following example from Noë 2004 to exemplify a DEUTS situation:

[P]erhaps the only way—or the only biologically possible way—to produce just the flavor sensation one enjoys when one sips a wine is by rolling a liquid across one's tongue. In that case, the liquid, the tongue, and the rolling action would be part of the physical substrate for the experience's occurrence.

Naturally, internalists want to claim that only a smaller part of this larger chain of activity constitutes the metaphysical basis of phenomenality. But how can they justify this in a non-question-begging way? Clark (2009) offers an empirically motivated reason for thinking the internalists might be right. While granting that intracerebral processes take their lead—as a matter of nomological fact—from interactions with worldly features, he argues that it may turn out that only the intracerebral activity is constitutive of phenomenality:

Perhaps conscious awareness is special among cognitive functions in so far as it requires (in us humans at least) certain information-accessing and information-integrating operations whose temporal scale makes neural (brain/CNS) processes (just as a matter of empirical fact) the only adequate 'vehicle'. (2009, p. 983)

In other words, Clark conjectures that it could turn out that—as a matter of fact—only internal neural processes are responsible for the "construction of conscious experience" (p. 984). Clark canvasses two possible ways of cashing out this idea: the construction of experience might be achieved by means of binding together sensibly coherent bodies of information or by means of attentional modulation that allows information to pass from perceptual buffers to working memory. Both of these proposals assume the existence of "bodies of neurally represented information" (p. 984). The upshot is that Clark can grant enactivists that experience only ever occurs in environment-involving circumstances while still holding on to, and empirically motivating, the idea that what is required for constituting consciousness is entirely internal and brain-bound. It might just turn out that what's in the head is both necessary and sufficient for phenomenality. In such a case, the causal supervenience base for phenomenality would be wide, involving the environment plus the brain, yet only the brain would play a constitutive role—so the metaphysics of phenomenality would be narrow after all.

It goes without saying that, from the perspective of REC, the two proposals that Clark considers are non-starters because they rely on the unrestricted CIC-ish idea of "neurally represented information." As we took pains to show in chapter 4, making good on the notion of "neurally represented information" depends on the success of a research tradition that is plagued with toxic debt, financed by loans it cannot pay back.

Can Clark's line of thought survive the subtraction of these CIC-ish commitments? Well, let us assume that there is a significant difference between the temporal signatures of the intracranial and wider, environment-involving interactions— and that only the former can provide the requisite fast activity. Of course this difference might be important; it might even be necessary for the existence of phenomenal experience. But there is no argument here to establish that it is sufficient. Hence, this consideration, by itself, provides no reason to think that phenomenality is, even probably, all in the head.

Something stronger is needed to establish—in a principled way—that *only* internal, neural activity is constitutive of phenomenality. The best way to achieve that is by invoking what may be the favorite philosophical argument for internalism about phenomenality. We call it the Argument from Shared Phenomenality. According to this argument, very similar phenomenology can occur in cases involving interactions with the environment (such as ordinary on-line perceiving) as well as in cases that don't involve such interactions. Phenomenal experience of the same kind that is enjoyed in on-line perception seems possible even when individuals are deprived of opportunities to interact with their environments—when external influences are either highly constrained or eliminated altogether. This possibility is established, *a priori*, by coherently imagining scenarios in which the relevant phenomenality occurs in strange circumstances with only limited or no interactions with an environment. Extravaganzas such as direct neural manipulations of envatted brains or marvelous quantum accidents that manage to replicate the relevant neural activity and hence the relevant phenomenology are supplied for this purpose. More mundanely, internalists also point to documented empirical cases of individuals dreaming, imagining, and suffering from "locked-in" syndrome or those in unresponsive conditions. There are important questions to be asked about how to evaluate the evidence for the commonality of phenomenal experience that is assumed when making such comparisons, and—indeed—how to determine the precise degree of similarity. For example, even if we suppose that individuals can enjoy phenomenal experience when there are diminished possibilities—or no possibility—for interacting with their environments, it is not obvious what we should say about the exact phenomenal character of such experiences. Even if it is not ruled out that individuals in such circumstances are experiencing something, it is far from clear what they are experiencing or how similar it is to what is experienced in richer, environment-involving cases. If REC is true, interpreting such evidence is even more difficult than many suppose, for then we must abandon the idea that sameness of phenomenality is a matter of the sameness of content—i.e., that such sameness has the kind of determinacy conferred by semantic or conceptual content. Consequently, questions can be raised about what it means to say or imagine that two experiences have identical or even similar phenomenal characters, or that they might be qualitatively indistinguishable.

But let us allow, for the sake of argument, that similar phenomenology can occur even in the complete absence of environmental interactions. What follows?

The assumption that phenomenology can be common in both wide and narrow cases has led internalists to maintain, for reasons of theoretical elegance, that the minimal supervenience base of phenomenal properties is narrow. They reason that if ever we can get by with less and still have phenomenology then it follows that such phenomenology supervenes on a narrow basis, even in circumstances in which there are environment-involving interactions. Concomitantly, they suppose that the laws of phenomenology, being common to all such cases, must be narrow (O'Regan and Block 2012).

However, even if the Argument from Shared Phenomenality has bite—even if the supervenience base of phenomenality is always brain-bound—it does not follow that the laws of phenomenology are, always and everywhere, narrow. What counts as a law—and certainly what counts as a law that yields adequate predictions and explanations—depends on the practical interests and purposes in play. Thus, focusing entirely on internal, brain-bound activity may be appropriate if one is interested only in producing or replicating phenomenality by limited or minimal means.

We can see the limitations of the narrow proposal if we consider cases in which we must practically produce phenomenology in everyday circumstances but not by means of direct neural intervention. Suppose that some person S wants to convey to a friend, F, what it is like to experience a late-Impressionist depiction of a rowboat. In the normal case, this is achieved only by indirectly manipulating the other's brain. S might do this by attempting to produce a painting in the late-Impressionist style and inviting F to look at it. To understand how this is possible—i.e., how the painting might be produced by S and appreciated by F in both cases by enactive and embodied means—is to understand the environment-involving activities of S and F. The latter can be explained only by invoking wide laws. By the same token, if we want to understand the place of phenomenality in nature—how it originally came to be, and why it has the features it has—we are likewise forced to widen our scope.

We have no objection to using thought experiments to clarify theoretical commitments, or to thinking that the minimal supervenience base for phenomenality may be brain-bound—i.e., that phenomenality can exist in the absence of its normal causes. But it is a great mistake to take the further step of inferring that a full understanding of the properties in question could ever be achieved by looking at neural properties alone, or that the best bet for understanding phenomenality is by narrowly focusing on such internal neural activity (see O'Regan and Block 2012). One need not assume that wide (contextual and historical) properties of a thing form part of its metaphysical essence—that is, one need not commit the genetic fallacy—to see that contextual and historical properties are crucial for answering genetic questions.

Besides, any convincing and thoroughgoing argument that rejects the "going wide" strategy on the grounds that it fails to get at the true essence of phenomenality will not justify giving special status to neural activity either. Arguably, the metaphysical train of thought that drives such essentialist reasoning is an express train that makes no stop at Station Neuroscience but instead goes directly to Proto-Panpsychism Central.[1] Failing to appreciate this important point has encouraged misguided attempts to develop a science of phenomenality that focuses exclusively on what goes on inside the head. Chalmers (2010) still envisions a science of consciousness that is essentially correlative—one that connects qualia with internal brain states. Yet, although he recognizes that robust scientific research into consciousness has blossomed in the past 16 years, he confesses to only limited progress in finding bridging principles to link first-person and third-person phenomena—as he construes them. Nevertheless, he tells us that "if one squints one can discern the possibility of a framework on the far horizon" (p. xvii).

Of course, although we balk at talk of qualia, we don't and needn't deny the value of purely neuroscientific investigations into the basis of phenomenality. They answer to certain needs.

Our point is that the strategy of going wide is necessary when trying to understand the phenomenality of experience in a wider context. Although frequently overlooked, the point we insist on is trivially true and it matters because going wide is the only way to properly understand phenomenality with respect to its natural and actual origins.

Enactivists are therefore right to emphasize the explanatory importance of understanding temporally extended sensorimotor interactions between organisms and their environments if we are to understand why token experiences have the particular phenomenal characters that they do (O'Regan 2011). This fits with the fact that specific patterns of interaction between organisms and their environments were originally and non-accidentally responsible for there being something-it-is-like to have certain kinds of experience. This can be so even if it should turn out not only that the phenomenal character of experiences causally (and hence explanatorily) supervenes on wide interactions but also that the latter non-instrumentally constitute the former. In the next section we consider a crucial and much-examined case in which an important philosophical purpose is served by going wide; we show how doing so allows us to avoid being sucked into trying to answer an impossible problem—the Hard Problem of Consciousness.

Impossible Problems and Real Solutions

In the passage quoted at the beginning of this chapter, Prinz finds it marvelous that enactivists could imagine—even momentarily—that, when it comes to closing the explanatory gap, a strategy of going wide has any advantage over more traditional approaches. (See also O'Regan and Block 2012.) Why? The story is familiar. Well, if there is an explanatory gap then there is a fundamental hole in our understanding of the relation of physicality to phenomenality (Levine 1983). To close the gap requires solving the Hard Problem of Consciousness (or the Hard Problem, for short). And offering a straight solution to that problem would demand showing how the phenomenal relates intelligibly to the physical (Chalmers 1995).

For many who feel the challenge of the Hard Problem, it looks as if there is no way to satisfactorily make sense of the relevant relation by any standard reductive means. The field of consciousness studies faces a foundational challenge. It has been argued that all standard forms of materialism are false (Chalmers 1996, 2010), because it seems to be impossible to reductively explain the phenomenal in terms of the physical broadly conceived. Arguments to establish this have been based on our apparent ability to coherently imagine philosophical zombies, phenomenal inverts, and strangely nurtured super-scientists (such as Jackson's Mary, who, despite knowing all the physical facts, does not know what it is like to see red).

The most obdurate response to the Hard Problem is that of Type A materialists. They deny the existence of any epistemic, metaphysical, or explanatory gap. For them, philosophical zombies are inconceivable, and, even when she is locked in her black-and-white room, there is nothing that Mary doesn't know about what it is like to experience redness. Although this needn't seem obvious, a wholly third-person approach—one that may involve complete knowledge of a correct physics—provides all that is required for understanding the phenomenal. Put this way, Type A materialism is indistinguishable from Type C materialism. (See Chalmers 2010.) Type C-ers hold that phenomenal zombies seem conceivable to us only because of our current state of knowledge; they are not conceivable in the limit. Type C types are really Type A types who add a "the check is in the mail" rider to their account.

When it comes to explaining consciousness, these strategies seem incapable of delivering the required goods, for the sort of explanations that can be provided by the natural sciences always and necessarily leave untouched what most needs explaining— i.e., the properties of what it is like to have a certain experience. These phenomenal properties of experiences cannot be accounted for by explanations cast in terms of functional, structural, or dynamic properties. Any attempt to explain the phenomenal aspects of experience by appealing to properties of the aforementioned kinds always fall short of what is required. Such explanations can only provide more detail about structure and dynamics; they never get at, never even mention, the requisite phenomenal features as such. Thus, those who hold out hope that explanatory or ontological reductions might be forthcoming by using only the standard resources of the physical sciences are out of luck. This is brought out most vividly if we imagine that, on the one side, there are qualia, such as phenomenal feels of red, and, on the other side, there are mere neural happenings. The qualia and the mere neural happenings appear to have nothing in common, and how a phenomenal experience of redness could ever be explained by accounts of neural activity seems utterly baffling. Intuitively, the problem is that "for any complex macroscopic structural or dynamical description of a system, one can conceive of that description's being satisfied without consciousness" (Chalmers 2010, p. 122). From this fact some have concluded that there is more to reality than is dreamt of, or posited by, modern-day materialist or physicalist philosophies. Assuming this to be so, they have accepted that the mere existence of phenomenal consciousness entails "extra ingredients" in reality—extra elements that exist above and beyond physical properties that account for phenomenality.

Qualia are extra entities that are, at best, nomologically associated with experiences of phenomenal consciousness. Thus, it may be that in our world physical properties must be related to qualia if there is to be phenomenal consciousness as a matter of natural law, but physical properties are not logically required for phenomenality. On this understanding of what is required to account for phenomenality the infamous explanatory gap cannot be closed by any reductive proposal in terms of neural structures, functions or dynamics. Nor would it help to look to activity and interactions that go beyond the brain, no matter how subtle, fine-grained, or wide ranging. Hence Prinz's puzzlement about what enactivists could hope to gain by going wide.

But Prinz-style puzzlement should dissipate if the Hard Problem proves to be a non-problem and if the enactivist strategy of going wide serves a different and more modest purpose than Prinz supposes. How might this work? Here is the recipe.

First, allow that phenomenal experiences admit of true physical descriptions, without assuming that such descriptions exhaust or fully characterize all aspects of their nature. Experiences can be enjoyed and truly described in ways that do not invoke the vocabulary of physics.

There is no ultimately privileged way of describing experiences that captures all their essential properties. However perfect physical science may become, its descriptions and its explanations will always be as conceptually limited and interest-sensitive as any other description or explanation. Even ideal physical descriptions don't provide a transparent window into every essential aspect of what they pick out in extension. Accepting this removes the temptation to think it is legitimate to expect that phenomenal descriptions might be inferred *a priori* from physical descriptions, but it still doesn't completely clear the air of explanatory mystery associated with the Hard Problem.

So, step two. Deny that there is a relation between the phenomenal and the physical that needs explaining. Consequently, solving the Hard Problem isn't just hard; it is impossible. The articulation of the Hard Problem serves the important function of exposing flaws in materialist thinking—those just mentioned above. It also shows that we need to rethink the standard picture of phenomenality in a quite fundamental way, giving up the notion of qualia. Nevertheless, practical wisdom dictates that we not try to give a straight solution to it. This is not to cop out. It's a waste of time to try to solve problems that cannot be solved.

What course do we recommend? Stick with REC and take phenomenality to be nothing but forms of activities—perhaps only neural—that are associated with environment-involving interactions. If that is so, there are not two distinct relata—the phenomenal and the physical—standing in a relation other than identity. Lastly, come to see that such identities cannot, and need not, be explained. If so, the Hard Problem totally disappears.

The best way to avoid being trapped in fruitless attempts to answer the Hard Problem—the way we recommend—has affinities with and is structurally similar to the escape route proposed by Type B materialists, who advocate the Phenomenal Concept Strategy (PCS). It is worth highlighting the differences between their exit strategy and ours to avoid confusion.

By far the most popular response to the Hard Problem has been to adopt some sort of Type B materialism—to accept that there is an epistemic and explanatory gap while denying the existence of an ontological gap. Philosophical zombies and their kin are conceivable, but this is put down to peculiar features of phenomenal concepts; nothing interesting about the metaphysics of consciousness follows from the fact that we can conceive of such monsters.

This is to opt for a non-explanatory physicalism. As a result, for Type B-ers the link between the physical and the phenomenal is thought to be epistemically primitive; one cannot deduce phenomenal truths *a priori* from known physical truths. That doesn't preclude physical facts' being all the facts. The phenomenal might just be the physical described differently—under a different guise or mode of presentation.

For Type B-ers, the trick is to "simply deny that there are two properties here" (Papineau 1993, p. 179–180). The Phenomenal Concept Strategy (which holds that the concepts of phenomenal properties are special in crucial respects) is one attempt to show how this denial of difference is possible and how it can be made plausible. Those who promote this strategy claim that the unique features of phenomenal concepts systematically foster, and ultimately explain, the illusion that phenomenal properties stand apart from all other properties, even though they don't.

A comparison helps. Public concepts of experience, such as 'redness' or 'itchiness', are thought to denote worldly properties that we perceive. In contrast, phenomenal concepts, such as 'seems red' or 'feels itchy', pick out properties of our experience of worldly properties and therefore are regarded as inherently first-personal (Papineau 2002; Tye 2009). Typically, it is imagined that such concepts are formed on the basis of re-enacting, having higher-order perceivings of or believings about first-order experiential states.

If there are such things as phenomenal concepts, and they are special in the ways described, then clearly they are irreducible to physical concepts. It is the irreducibility of phenomenal concepts to any other sort of concept that provides a general strategy for dealing with thought experiments that are designed to bother reductive naturalists. Thus, the Phenomenal Concept Strategy allows one to argue that it only seems as if philosophical zombies or phenomenal inverts are metaphysically possible because they are coherently conceivable (or at least ideally so). Such oddities can be imagined because we can coherently conceptually imagine that phenomenal properties are distinct from all other properties, even if they cannot be. Similarly, it only seems that Mary doesn't know all the facts. In truth, she does know everything factual that could be known, but she knows some of these facts under limited descriptions, lacking a special mode of presentation because she lacks the relevant phenomenal concepts.

Put simply, the Phenomenal Concept Strategy licenses the following sort of inference:

If feelings are one and the same as brain states, then brain states don't 'generate' a further realm of feelings (or 'give rise to' them, or 'accompany' them, or 'are correlated with' them). Rather, brain states are the feelings. (Papineau 2002, p. 3)

In line with this, the best policy for dealing with the Hard Problem is avoidance. The tactic of not allowing for metaphysical difference pays off because "as soon as you suppose that conscious states are distinct from material states, then some very puzzling questions become unavoidable" (ibid., p. 2).

Importantly, the Type B way of dealing with the Hard Problem refuses to take it seriously—but it does so while denying that concepts of experience simply reduce to physical concepts (broadly conceived). Thus it avoids commitment, embraced by more hard-core Type A physicalists, to the idea that the facts of experience can be deduced *a priori* simply by knowing the relevant physical facts.

To be precise, it might be possible to know—on the basis of knowing that certain identities hold, at least in the actual world—that a certain type of phenomenality will obtain when a certain activity (as described in the language of physics or neuroscience) obtains. Of course, it doesn't follow—even if such entailments hold—that we can get from descriptions that pick out phenomenal experiences to a sense of what it is like to have such experiences. It is certainly not possible to infer, from a physical description of an activity alone, what it is like to undergo such an activity.

Not only do defenders of the Phenomenal Concept Strategy deny the possibility of getting at what it is like to have experiences through such *a priori* entailments; they also rightly observe that any self-respecting identity theorist must resist trying to explain how phenomenality is generated by brain activity—that is, trying to answer the question of how purely physical activity manages to "give rise" to phenomenality.

Although the basic strategy of the Type B solution is attractively straightforward, its particular implementation by invoking the Phenomenal Concept Strategy is limited in crucial respects; it embeds problematic assumptions. Several prominent critics doubt the tenability of the Phenomenal Concept Strategy because they question the existence of concepts of the special sort it posits. (See Prinz 2007 and Tye 2009.) We agree. In line with REC, we cannot accept the existence of special phenomenal concepts, nor can we accept standard stories about how they are formed through first-personal acts of introspection. For example, according to Chalmers phenomenal concepts arise when a subject attends to the quality of an experience and forms a concept based wholly on the attention to the quality, "taking up" the quality into the concept. This is part and parcel of Chalmers' assumption that experiences constitute part of the content of our introspective reports. Thus, "the content of a phenomenal concept . . . is partly constituted by an underlying phenomenal quality" (Chalmers 2003, p. 235; see also pp. 233 and 236–239).

By contrast, we hold that anything that might answer to the name 'phenomenal concept' will be a public concept that allows us to talk about the 'redness of red'—the redness of red experiences—only because it derives from and is parasitic on the public concept 'red'. In line with the Scaffolded Mind Hypothesis (described in the preceding chapter), the very possibility of conceptual meaning, even in the case of phenomenality, requires an inter-subjective space.[2] Acknowledging this entails no denial of the existence of nonconceptual, noncontentful experiences with phenomenal properties associated with basic minds. (Normally, these phenomenal experiences take the form of our primary engagements with others and with worldly things and their features.) However, it is to insist that our facility with concepts about such experiences is parasitic on a more basic literacy in making ordinary claims about public, worldly items. Non-viciously but importantly, the acquisition of such conceptual abilities depends on being able to have and share basic experiences with others. We therefore reach the same conclusion as Tye ("There is really *nothing* special about phenomenal concepts"—Tye 2009, p. 56), but by a different route.

Now that we have clarified the crucial respect in which our approach to the Hard Problem differs from the approach of Type B-ers who rely on the Phenomenal Concept Strategy, there is one remaining issue to resolve: It doesn't seem good enough simply to insist on phenomeno-physical identities and to stipulate that there is no need to explain them. Crucially, making room for the mere possibility of identities does nothing, by itself, to motivate belief in the proposed identities. At most, it makes space for their possible truth, securing the barest logical possibility that the putative identities may hold.

Standard Type B offerings therefore fail to face up to the root challenge of the Hard Problem—they fail to address worries about the intelligibility of making certain identity claims head on. They do nothing to make the making of such claims plausible. The punch line is that to make a credible case for phenomeno-physical identity claims it is necessary to deal with—to explain away—appearances of difference in a more satisfactory way than by offering mere stipulations.

This is precisely where the enactivist strategy of going wide shows its worth. To see why, it is important to be more precise about the worry concerning unexplained identities. Some Type B-ers point out that it makes no more sense to ask why the phenomenal and physical are the same than it does to ask why Clark Kent is Superman. The worry is that saying only this underestimates the intellectual barrier that has to be overcome in order to motivate belief in phenomeno-physical identities. This is because, whereas both Clark Kent and Superman belong to a common category (that of persons), there is apparently no such common category that can ground the phenomeno-physical identity claims.

Moreover, critics complain that an appeal to unexplained identities in this domain simply won't do, since identities in other domains can be deduced from more basic truths (see p. 117). Chalmers asserts:

Identities are ontologically primitive, but they are not epistemically primitive. . . . Identities are typically implied by underlying truths that do not involve identities. The identities between genes and DNA and water and H2O are implied by . . . underlying truths. . . . Once a subject knows all the truths about DNA and its role in reproduction and development, for example, the subject will be in a position to deduce that genes are DNA. (2010, p. 244)

Like Tye (2009), we believe that holding out hope for *a priori* deductive explanations of identities in terms of underlying truths of microphysical and indexical facts—those of the sort to which Chalmers alludes—is "no more than wishful thinking" (p. 57). To suppose otherwise is to buy into mistaken and exaggerated assumptions about the nature of explanations that establish identities in science generally.

Certainly it is possible to explain, transparently, how chemical molecules are composed of particular types of atoms with specific atomic weights. At the atomic level, we can specify all the necessary conditions for the formation of particular chemical molecules. The physics entails the chemistry. This is because a chemical compound is nothing but an arrangement of certain kinds of atoms, in the right numbers, linked together in a specific way. It is an easy matter to motivate identity claims in this domain because chemistry and physics belong to a common conceptual framework, despite their divergent explanatory interests and methods. In this light, it is no surprise that the relations between the entities described in chemistry and physics are the paradigm of intelligible inter-theoretic relations. It is not a puzzle to understand how the relevant identities can hold. Yet this ideal is rarely realized, even in science. Reductions by strict nomological deduction are, at best, the exception, not the rule. They are not generally required for motivating belief in identities.

Most contemporary philosophers of science hold that reduction should not be thought of as requiring strict deductive-nomological deductions. It is generally thought to be sufficient for achieving reduction if the "image of the higher order theory," or more specifically its explanatory and predictive resources, can be preserved by the lower-level theory (Churchland 1989, p. 49; see also pp. 153–154). Still, there are those who regard even this as being too quasi-Nagelian in spirit (Smith 1992, pp. 28–29, 33–35). It is possible to opt for even softer versions of inter-theoretical relations while assuming the existence of relevant identity claims.

In line with this more liberal thinking about how identities can be established, we think it is a fool's errand to try to explain, establish or make credible phenomeno-physical identities in the way Chalmers demands. It is reasonable, and possible, to motivate belief in such identities by other, softer means.[3] This requires making two moves. We can advance in our thinking about phenomeno-physical identities only by (1) appropriately relaxing our explanatory demands (as just argued) and (2) reconceiving the nature of phenomenality by adjusting our conceptual filters.

In line with the second of these moves, we suggest fiddling with our conception of what phenomenality is.[4] Like other enactivists, we reject the standard ways of characterizing the 'phenomeno' side of phenomeno-physical identities. The difficulty with other existing conceptions of phenomenal properties is that their advocates are wedded to confused pictures of what is to be identified, when they imagine the *relata* to be qualia and brain states. In this context—and not in a bid to provide a straight solution to the Hard Problem—the enactivist strategy of "going wide" once again proves useful. For the plausibility of the proposed identities looks entirely different, and far less contrived, if it is assumed that the phenomenal character of experiences must, ultimately, be understood by appealing to interactions between experiencers and aspects of their environments. This holds true, even if in the end it should turn out that phenomenality is nothing other than neural activity associated with wider organismic activities.

These proposals are in tune with the unpolished way that we ordinarily speak about, identify, and characterize the phenomenal properties of experiences. Naturally occurring "what it is like" or "what it feels like" illocutions take activities as their natural objects. When we describe phenomenal experience, we cannot help but mention environment-involving interactions. Thus we talk of what it is like to feel the softness of sponge by squishing it, what it is like to savor the distinct flavor of a 14-year old Clynelish single malt, and what it is like to taste the cold wetness of a snowflake on one's tongue. We do not normally (at least, not without a good deal of prompting and direction) speak about what it is like to experience the "redness of red" (where this property is thought to mentally denote being a special, private object of our mental acquaintance) without assuming such activities lie in the background.

Enactivists foreground the ways in which environment-involving activities are required for understanding and conceiving of phenomenality. They abandon attempts to explain phenomeno-physical identities in deductive terms for attempts to motivate belief in such identities by reminding us of our common ways of thinking and talking about phenomenal experience. Continued hesitance to believe in such identities stems largely from the fact that experiences—even if understood as activities—are differently encountered by us: sometimes we live them through embodied activity and sometimes we get at them only descriptively.

In the end, like proponents of the Phenomenal Concept Strategy, we do not offer a straight solution to the Hard Problem. Nevertheless, we try to do more than simply stipulate that qualia are identical to brain states. We couch and motivate phenomeno-physical identity claims differently—providing more illuminating and convincing grounds for believing in such identities. Rather than presenting science and philosophy with an agenda of solving impossible problems, this approach liberates both science and philosophy to pursue goals they are able to achieve.

Casting back, we are now in a position to reply to Prinz's remark, cited in our preface, that "radicalism may be good for politics, but it's bad for science" (2009, p. 419).We say: Whatever value radicalism may have for politics, not only science but also philosophy benefits by radicalizing enactivism.

Notes

Chapter 1

1. All contemporary enactivists endorse this claim. For example, Thompson (2007, p. 128) tells us that "life and mind share a set of basic organizational properties, and the organizational properties distinctive of mind are an enriched version of those fundamental to life. Mind is life-like and life is mind-like." According to Noë (2009, p. 41), "What biology brings into focus is the living being, but where we discern life, we have everything we need to discern mind. . . . You can't both acknowledge the existence of the organism and at the same time just view it as just a locus of processes or physiochemical mechanisms."

2. Talk of the body here does not denote the "body (understood literally)," whatever exactly that is supposed to mean. And it certainly doesn't pick out "the whole physical body, minus the brain." (See Goldman and de Vignemont 2009, p. 154.)

3. This phrase, much invoked by enactivists, comes from a poem by Antonio Machado. (See Varela, Thompson, and Rosch 1991, chapter 11; Thompson 2007, p. 180; Noë 2009, chapter 5.)

4. For some authors this ruling applies to all forms of mentality. Thus they hold that even the phenomenal characters of experiences reduce to, or are exhausted by, the contentful properties of mental states. If that is so, absolutely nothing mental escapes CIC's net.

5. The idea that intellectualists might use enactivist ideas to accessorize in this way is discussed in chapter 1 of Shapiro 2011.

6. This is to accept that "representational uses of language . . . require a context . . . the exercise of techniques for going on in the same way, and shared sense of the obvious and the certain" (Williams 2010, p. 3).

7. As Gauker (2011, p. 5) observes, "It is commonplace to speak of content Platonistically, as it were an object in Plato's heaven, distinct from things in brains. Speaking in that way, we may say that your judgement and my judgement possess or bear or express the same content."

Chapter 2

1. On page 940 of their landmark 2001 paper, O'Regan and Noë present the central idea of their new approach as the claim that "vision is a mode of exploration of the world that is mediated by knowledge of what we call sensorimotor contingencies." Elaborating this on page 946, they write: "Visual experience is a mode of activity involving practical knowledge about currently possible behaviours and associated sensory consequences. Visual experience rests on know how, the possession of skills."

2. For example, O'Regan and Noë (2001) speak of brains' being able to "accurately judge whether an object is stationary" (p. 949), having "to assume that the observer was not seeing" (p. 950), and having "to conclude that the object was not being seen" (p. 951). Equally, they talk of perceivers' knowing "that if you were to move your eyes slightly leftwards, the object would shift one way on your retina, but if you were to move your eye rightwards, the object would shift the other way" (p. 949).

3. Of course, the knowledge in question may still be essentially practical in an uninteresting sense if it turns out that all practical knowledge reduces to propositional knowledge, as Stanley and Williamson (2001) propose.

4. We agree with Clark (2008b, p. 175) that it is not necessary to "appeal to predictions (or expectations) concerning the next sensory stimulation directly and exhaustively to explain (subpersonally) or even characterize (personally) perceptual experience."

5. Noë (2012) has revised his position and now appears to be going the REC way. "To be conscious of something," he writes, "is not to depict it, or to represent it. To perceive something is not to consume it, just as it isn't a matter of constructing, within our brains or minds, a model or picture or representation of the world without. There is no need. The world is right there and it suffices" (p. 21).

Chapter 3

1. This intellectualist way of understanding the basic nature of minds taps into a long tradition stretching back at least as far as Plato; revived by Descartes in the modern era, it regained ascendancy most recently through the work of Chomsky. As Noë (2009, p. 98) observes, "What these views have in common—and what they have bequeathed to cognitive science—is the idea that we are, in our truest nature, thinkers. It is this intellectualist background that shapes the way cognitive scientists think about human beings."

2. It is perhaps understandable that in seeking to make sense of this cognitive activity we are naturally inclined to assume the existence of representations that "include not only 'commands' and 'calculations', but also 'if-then' and other logical operations. This shows how it seems impossible to make sense of cerebral control—requisition and modification—of motor programs, to describe them in such a way that they deliver what is needed while avoiding anthropomorphisms." (Tallis 2003, p. 65) The problem is that "attributing to the brain, or parts of it, or neural circuits, the ability to do things that we, whole human beings, most certainly cannot do, seems unlikely to solve the puzzle" (ibid., p. 65).

3. These could include "grasping, seizing, pulling, plucking, picking, pinching, pressing, patting, poking, prodding, fumbling, squeezing, crushing, throttling, punching, rubbing, scratching, groping, stroking, caressing, fingering, drumming, shaping, lifting, flicking, catching, throwing, and much besides" (Tallis 2003, p. 22).

Chapter 4

1. Wheeler—a prominent spokesperson for action-oriented representa-tions—explicitly endorses this assumption. Confessing that "the rela-tionship between decoupleability . . . and representation seems to get murkier every time [he] think[s] about it," he says he is "convinced that decoupleability is not necessary for minimal representation" (2008, p. 372) Abandoning a decoupleabilty constraint for action-oriented repre-sentations is a smart move in any case. For a full discussion of this topic, see chapter 3 of Chemero 2009.

2. Notably, Chemero (2009) holds that the centrifugal governor is not a computer even though it can be regarded as a representational device. In this respect he doesn't break faith with the conclusion of Van Gelder's original analysis (1995).

3. Thus "If we suppose that, through selection, an internal indicator acquired a biological function, the function to indicate something about the animal's surroundings, then we can say that this internal structure represents." (Dretske 1988, p. 94)

4. This fits with what Dretske (1995) writes elsewhere when he speaks of what a device says or means or represents, though he hedges his bets by using scare quotes when describing the acts of communication at this level. For example: "A playground teeter-totter's position stands in the same relation to the children playing on it that a beam balance stands to the objects whose weights it has the function to compare. The behavior of the balance "says" or represents something about the objects on it. It "says" that one is heavier than the other. The teeter-tot-ter does not." (1995, p. 30)

5. Dretske speaks of "a signal's propositional content" (1981, p. 68) and makes clear his commitments in this regard when he asks "What is the content of this signal? What is the message?" (ibid., p. 69). He holds that the informational content of a signal can be captured by descrip-tions that focus on predicate expressions, such as ". . . is F." Accordingly, "The informational content of a signal is being expressed in the form 's

is F' where the letter s is understood to be an indexical or demonstrative element referring to some item at the source." (ibid., p. 66)

6. Early analytic philosophers were at home with the view that the world is ultimately and literally composed, at least in part, by "propositions." These were conceived of as bedrock Platonic entities—mentionable "terms" that, when standing in the right complex relations, constitute judgeable objects of thought. In commenting on Russell's version of this idea, Makin underscores the features that parallel many of the properties that Dretske demands of informational content: "[W]ith propositions, it is crucial to bear in mind that they are not, nor are they abstracted from, symbolic or linguistic or psychological entities. . . . On the contrary, *they are conceived as fundamentally independent of both language and mind. Propositions are first and foremost the entities that enter into logical relations of implication, and hence also the primary bearers of truth. . . .* 'Truth' and 'implication' apply, in their primary senses, to propositions and only derivatively to the sentences expressing them" (2000, p. 11, emphasis added).

7. Others too have noticed this. For example, Ramsey comments on the peculiar features of the quasi-semantic indication relation as follows: "Dretske and many authors are somewhat unclear on the nature of this relation. While it is fairly clear what it means to say that state A nomically depends upon state B, it is much less clear how such a claim is supposed to translate into the claim that A is an indicator of B, or how we are to understand expressions like 'information flow' and 'information carrying.'" (2007, p. 133)

8. This should not be a controversial claim. After all, there is nothing special about brain states that distinguishes them, in any relevant respect, from other kinds of occurring states of affairs. Bits of the world do not indicate other bits of the world. After all, even Fodor accepts that "the world can't be its own best representation because the world doesn't represent anything; least of all itself" (2009, p. 15).

9. Even if we imagine that natural indicators of the sort Dretske posits might exist, their informational content will be indeterminate with

respect to any analytically nested information. Jacob (1997) helpfully labels this nesting problem "the transitivity problem." (For a discussion, see chapter 2 of Hutto 1999.)

Chapter 5

1. Despite rejecting them as inadequate for this task, Burge (2010, p. 9) admits that "the reductionist projects do invoke a broad but recognizable use of the term 'representation'. Roughly, on this use, one set of phenomena represents another set if there is a systematic correlation between the sets. One can add that the representing set is the causal product of the represented set, or is reliably associated with the represented set. And one can go further, maintaining that the representing set functions to enable an individual to cope with the represented set. These ways of using the term 'representation' occur in psychology as well as philosophy. They are so broad that they apply to the states of furnaces, plants, and bacteria."

2. Some interesting consequences follow for Fodor in the light of his other stated commitments. Presumably, for Fodor registering is not any kind of mental activity, for he tells us that "the mark of the mental is its intensionality; that's to say that mental states have content. . . . [O]nly what's literally and unmetaphorically mental has content." (Fodor 2009, p. 14) But if intensional content *is* the mark of the mental, and only what has such content is mental, then states of subjects that merely covary with environmental ones, those that merely register, don't qualify as mental (by Fodor's own criterion). At best they have intentionality. Still, whether or not registering qualifies as mental, Fodor holds that "the notion of carrying information about X seems to offer a way of representing X without representing it as anything," and that "assuming an informational construal of the given allows for representation *of* that isn't representation *as*" (2008b, p. 182). To suppose that the mere existence of information-carrying states suffices for the existence of a kind of nonconceptual mental representation is surely a radical departure from standard thinking about what is minimally required to qualify as a representational state. But in any case, on a REC

view informationally sensitive responding—which comes closest to what Fodor understands registering to be—doesn't qualify as any sort of representing, not even representing of a nonconceptual sort.

3. Might the relevant debt be paid another way? Carruthers (2009, pp. 170–171) observes, after all, that "few researchers in cognitive science actually rely on an informational account of representation in their own work. Most adopt some or other variety of inferential or conceptual role semantics (e.g. Block 1986), according to which what a symbol represents depends (at least partly) upon the use that the rest of the cognitive system is apt to make of that symbol. This is probably wise since purely informational accounts of intentional content face notorious difficulties." One reason we omit examination of this possibility from this book is that the objections to this line of reply are well rehearsed. (See chapter 2 of Hutto 1999.) It is not at all clear what contribution any imagined symbol might make to the putative content of other imagined symbols unless it is assumed that the symbols in question already have content. To get this sort of account off the ground it must be assumed that the allegedly content-conferring symbols in the network already possess at least some content—content that is somehow, therefore, independent of their roles in the system. Unless it is explained how this initial content gets to be in place, "the semantic properties . . . are assumed, not explained" (Fodor 1991, p. 46). Without supplement, appeals to conceptual or functional role semantics are, for this reason, explanatory non-starters.

4. Fodor chides Chomsky for his loose talk of "mental organs" on the ground that it fails to capture what is most distinctive about cognitivist proposals—i.e., that the postulated mechanisms must be *characterized* by their *representational* contents. Thus, to be a fully paid up cognitivist is to stand fast in one's belief in the existence of "domain specific propositional attitudes[,] not [just] . . . domain specific 'devices'" (Fodor 2001, p. 107).

5. Here Gauker buys into what he takes to be the consensus view among today's philosophers: "that what we perceive is normally objects and their properties outside of ourselves and not our own sensory experiences" (2011, p. 64).

6. Perceptual content would, on this view, be a kind of sub-personal content. But then the Accessibility Assumption would be violated, since "we" would be unable to get at perceptual contents without—if this were possible at all—engaging in special kinds of scientific investigation.

Chapter 6

1. Gauker holds that "thinking takes place in brains, and, as far as we know only in brains" (2011, p. 146).

2. Gauker (2011, p. 196) acknowledges that the definitions of normal function he appeals to in order to put the meat on the bones of his account are "inspired by the work of Ruth Millikan (1993)."

3. In a nutshell: "Biological functions are functions that have ultimately to do with contributing to fitness for evolutionary success. Fitness is very clearly a practical value. It is a state that is ultimately grounded in benefit of its effects for survival for reproduction. Explanations that appeal to biological function are explanations of the practical (fitness) value of a trait or system. But accuracy is not *in itself* a practical value." (Burge 2010, p. 301) Mother Nature satisfices, she does not optimize. Thus, "being fitted to successful evolution is a matter of functioning well enough to contribute to survival and reproduction. Well enough often coincides with veridicality. But even coincidence is not identity. Biological explanations of function explain a different feature of reality than do explanations of veridicality and error." (ibid., p. 303)

4. Burge identifies a set of epistemic natural norms that apply to perception: "(i) to perceive things as they are; (ii) to perceive as well as the perceptual system can, given its natural limitations, its input, and its environmental circumstances; (iii) to be reliably veridical; (iv) to be reliably veridical and to perceptually represent as well as possible given the perceptual system's natural limitations, its input, and its environmental circumstances" (Burge 2010, p. 312).

5. Burge is obdurate that perceptual constancies are sufficient for perceptual representations, but he only conjectures that the former might be necessary for the latter (2010, p. 413).

6. These capacities are, however, differently supported at the neural level. The neurons associated with frog's monocular perceptual capacities are only good enough to enable it to orient toward prey; thus, "it is thought that more precise localization is carried out by different sets of tectal and thalmatic neurons" (Neander 2006, p. 181).

7. In summarizing her views, Neander openly admits that, although she is aware of radical critiques of mainstream cognitive science, her conclusions "are conditional on the assumption that a theory of mental content should meet the needs of mainstream cognitive science" (2006, p. 191).

8. In Neander's shorthand, +T5(2) is a high frequency of action potential activity in a T5(2) cell in the optic tectum of anurans—which she takes, on balance, to be the best candidate for what "might be the 'prey-recognition' neurons" (2006, p. 178).

9. Chalmers holds that experiences enjoy a veritable smorgasbord of content—there is Russellian content, there is Fregean content, and there is Edenic content. To tell the full story would require giving detail about each. Chalmers presents this pluralism as unproblematic because he characterizes Russellian contents as extensions and Fregean contents—modes of presentation—as conditions on extensions. Ultimately, owing to problems with Russellian representationalism, he favors a Fregean account of phenomenal content.

Chapter 7

1. There are rare exceptions—see, e.g., Chemero 2009, Di Paolo 2009, and Steiner 2010.

2. Adams and Aizawa (2010, p. 581) are clear that for them talk of intrinsic content just equates to talk of underived content.

3. We agree with Menary (2010b, p. 232) that "we need to reconceive the mind on both bodily and environmental grounds. For example, integrationists take the manipulation of external vehicles to be a prerequisite for higher cognition and embodied engagement to be a precondition for these manipulative abilities."

Chapter 8

1. Coleman, for example, now defends the proto-panpsychist view as the natural and logical superior development of panpsychism, having previously held that the latter "answers the call of the deepest and most sober of metaphysical needs" (2009 p. 84). As Coleman observed, "if God didn't create a panpsychist world, then there's a fair chance that he wishes he had done so, or will do next time around" (p. 83).

2. By contrast, Chalmers thinks that there is a meaningful, contentful private language for expressing phenomenal concepts. Hence, he admits that his view is just the sort of view "that Wittgenstein directed his private language argument against. The nature of the private language argument is contested, so in response I can say only that I have seen no reconstruction of it that provides a strong case against the view I have laid out." (Chalmers 2003, p. 241)

3. Of course, this might count as explaining in a less demanding, non-Chalmeresque sense. (For a statement and an application of this point in the context of sensorimotor enactivism, see Myin and O'Regan 2009, p. 196.)

4. This is so despite the fact that our interest is always, ultimately, in the phenomenon of phenomenality itself—"the worldly property" (Carruthers 1996, p. 147).

References

Adams, F. 2010. Embodied cognition. *Phenomenology and the Cognitive Sciences* 9: 619–628.

Adams, F., and Aizawa, K. 2001. The bounds of cognition. *Philosophical Psychology* 14: 43–64.

Adams, F., and Aizawa, K. 2008. *The Bounds of Cognition*. Blackwell.

Adams, F., and Aizawa, K. 2010. The value of cognitivism for thinking about extended cognition. *Phenomenology and the Cognitive Sciences* 9: 579–603.

Araújo, D., and Davids, K. 2011. What exactly is acquired during skill acquisition? *Journal of Consciousness Studies* 18 (3–4): 7–23.

Bechtel, W. 1988. *Philosophy of Mind: An Overview for Cognitive Science*. Erlbaum.

Bechtel, W. 2001. Representations from neural systems to cognitive systems. In *Philosophy and the Neurosciences*, ed. W. Bechtel et al. Blackwell.

Beer, R. D. 1996. Toward the evolution of dynamical neural networks for minimally cognitive behavior. In *From Animals to Animats 4: Proceedings of the Fourth International Conference on Simulation of Adaptive Behavior*, ed. P. Maes et al. MIT Press.

Beer, R. D. 1998. Framing the debate between computational and dynamical approaches to cognitive science. *Behavioral and Brain Sciences* 21: 630.

Beer, R. D. 2000. Dynamical approaches to cognitive science. *Trends in Cognitive Sciences* 4 (3): 91–99.

Bermudez, J. L. 2011. The force-field puzzle and mindreading in non-human primates. *Review of Philosophy and Psychology* 2: 397–410.

Block, N. 2005. Review of Alva Noë, *Action in perception*. *Journal of Philosophy* 102: 259–272.

Branquinho, J. 2001. *The Foundations of Cognitive Science*. Oxford University Press.

Brooks, R. 1991a. New approaches to robotics. *Science* 253: 1227–1232.

Brooks, R. 1991b. Intelligence without representation. *Artificial Intelligence* 47: 139–159.

Burge, T. 2010. *The Origins of Objectivity*. Oxford University Press.

Carruthers, P. 1996. *Language, Thought and Consciousness*. Cambridge University Press.

Carruthers, P. 2009. Mindreading underlies metacognition. *Behavioral and Brain Sciences* 32: 121–182.

Chalmers, D. 1995. Facing up to the problem of consciousness. *Journal of Consciousness Studies* 2 (3): 200–219.

Chalmers, D. 1996. *The Conscious Mind*. Oxford University Press.

Chalmers, D. 2003. The content and epistemology of phenomenal belief. In *Consciousness: New Philosophical Perspectives*, ed. Q. Smith and A. Jokic. Oxford University Press.

Chalmers, D. 2010. *The Character of Consciousness*. Oxford University Press.

Chemero, A. 2009. *Radical Embodied Cognitive Science*. MIT Press.

Churchland, P. M. 2007. The evolving fortunes of eliminative materialism. In *Contemporary Debates in Philosophy of Mind*, ed. B. McLaughlin and J. Cohen. Blackwell.

Chomsky, N. 1988. *Language and Problems of Knowledge: The Managua Lectures*. MIT Press.

Clark, A. 2001. *Mindware. An Introduction to the Philosophy of Cognitive Science*. Oxford University Press.

Clark, A. 2008a. Pressing the flesh: A tension in the study of the embodied, embedded Mind? *Philosophy and Phenomenological Research* 76: 37–59.

Clark, A. 2008b. *Supersizing the Mind: Embodiment, Action, and Cognitive Extension*. Oxford University Press.

Clark, A. 2009. Spreading the joy? Why the machinery of consciousness is (probably) still in the head. *Mind* 118 (472): 964–993.

Clark, A., and Chalmers, C. 1998. The extended mind. *Analysis* 58: 7–19.

Cohen, M. A., and Dennett, D. C. 2011. Consciousness cannot be separated from function. *Trends in Cognitive Sciences* 15: 358–364.

Coleman, S. 2009. Mind under matter. In *Mind That Abides*, ed. D. Skrbina and G. Globus. John Benjamins.

Colombetti, G. 2010. Enaction, sense-making, and emotion. In *Enaction: Toward a New Paradigm for Cognitive Science*, ed. J. Stewart et al. MIT Press.

Crane, T. 2009. Is perception a propositional attitude? *Philosophical Quarterly* 59: 452–469.

Cummins, R., Blackmon, J., Bird, D., Lee, A., and Roth, M. 2006. Representation and unexploited content. In *Teleosemantics*, ed. G. Macdonald and D. Papineau. Oxford University Press.

Currie, G. 2010. *Narratives and Narrators: A Philosophy of Stories*. Oxford University Press.

Cosmelli, D., and Thompson, E. 2010. Embodiment or envatment? Reflections on the bodily basis of consciousness. In *Enaction: Toward a New Paradigm for Cognitive Science*, ed. J. Stewart et al. MIT Press.

Dennett, D. C. 1988. Quining qualia. In *Consciousness in Modern Science*, ed. A. Marcel and E. Bisiach. Oxford University Press.

Dennett, D. C. 1991. *Consciousness Explained*. Penguin.

Di Paolo, E. A. 2009. Extended life. *Topoi* 28: 9–21.

Dietrich, E., and Markman, A. 2003. Discrete thoughts: Why cognition must use discrete representations. *Mind & Language* 18: 95–119.

Dretske, F. 1981. *Knowledge and the Flow of Information.* MIT Press.

Dretske, F. 1988. *Explaining Behavior: Reasons in a World of Causes.* MIT Press.

Dretske, F. 1995. *Naturalizing the Mind.* MIT Press.

Evans, G. 1982. *The Varieties of Reference.* Oxford University Press.

Fodor, J. A. 1983. *The Modularity of Mind.* MIT Press.

Fodor, J. A. 1990. *A Theory of Content and Other Essays.* MIT Press.

Fodor, J. A. 2001. Doing without what's within. *Mind* 110: 99–148.

Fodor, J. A. 2008a. Against Darwinism. *Mind & Language* 23: 1–24.

Fodor, J. A. 2008b. *LOT 2: The Language of Thought Revisited.* Oxford University Press.

Fodor, J. A. 2009. Where is my mind? *London Review of Books*, 12 February.

Francheschini, N., Pichon, J. M., and Blanes, C. 1992. From insect vision to robot vision. *Philosophical Transactions of the Royal Society of London. Series B, Biological Sciences* 337: 283–294.

Freeman, W. 1991. The physiology of perception. *Scientific American* 264 (2): 78–85.

Garzón, F. C. 2008. Towards a general theory of antirepresentationalism. *British Journal for the Philosophy of Science* 59 (3): 259–292.

Gauker, C. 2011. *Words and Images. An Essay on the Origin of Ideas.* Oxford University Press.

Gauker, C. 2012. Perception without propositions. In *Philosophical Perspectives 26: Philosophy of Mind*, ed. J. Hawthorne and J. Turner. Blackwell.

Gendler, T. 2008. Alief in action (and reaction). *Mind & Language* 23 (5): 552–585.

Goldman, A. 2009. Mirroring, simulating and mindreading. *Mind & Language* 24 (2): 235–252.

Goldman, A., and de Vignemont, F. 2009. Is social cognition embodied? *Trends in Cognitive Sciences* 13 (4): 154–159.

Godfrey-Smith, P. 2006. Mental representation, naturalism and teleosemantics. In *Teleosemantics*, ed. G. Macdonald and D. Papineau. Oxford University Press.

Godfrey-Smith, P. 2007. Information in biology. In *The Cambridge Guide to the Philosophy of Biology*, ed. D. L. Hull and M. Ruse. Cambridge University Press.

Griffiths, P. 2001. Genetic information: A metaphor in search of a theory. *Philosophy of Science* 68 (3): 394–412.

Gunther, Y. 2003. General introduction. In *Essays on Nonconceptual Content*, ed. Y. Gunther. MIT Press.

Haugeland, J. 1998. Mind embodied and embedded. In *Having Thought: Essays in the Metaphysics of Mind*. Harvard University Press.

Heck, R. G., Jr. 2007. Are there different kinds of content? In *Contemporary Debates in Philosophy of Mind*, ed. B. McLaughlin and J. Cohen. Blackwell.

Hill, C. S. 2009. *Consciousness*. Cambridge University Press.

Hurley, S. 1998. *Consciousness in Action*. Harvard University Press.

Hurley, S. 2008. The shared circuits model: How control, mirroring and simulation can enable imitation and mindreading. *Behavioral and Brain Sciences* 31 (1): 1–22.

Hurley, S. 2010. The varieties of externalism. In *The Extended Mind*, ed. R. Menary. MIT Press.

Hurley, S., and Noë, A. 2003. Neural plasticity and consciousness. *Biology and Philosophy* 18: 131–168.

Hutto, D. D. 1999. *The Presence of Mind*. John Benjamins.

Hutto, D. D. 2000. *Beyond Physicalism*. John Benjamins.

Hutto, D. D. 2003/2006. *Wittgenstein and the End of Philosophy: Neither Theory nor Therapy*. Palgrave Macmillan.

Hutto, D. D. 2005. Knowing what? Radical versus conservative enactivism. *Phenomenology and the Cognitive Sciences* 4: 389–405.

Hutto, D. D. 2006. Turning hard problems on their heads. *Phenomenology and the Cognitive Sciences* 5 (1): 75–88.

Hutto, D. D. 2008. *Folk Psychological Narratives: The Socio-Cultural Basis of Understanding Reasons*. MIT Press.

Hutto, D. D. 2009. Mental representation and consciousness. In *Encyclopedia of Consciousness*, ed. W. Banks. Elsevier.

Jacob, P. 1997. *What Minds Can Do*. Cambridge University Press.

Jackson, F., and Pettit, P. 1993. Some content is narrow. In *Mental Causation*, ed. J. Heil and A. Mele. Oxford University Press.

James, W. 1909. *The Meaning of Truth*. Longman, Green.

Kelly, S. 2001/2003. The non-conceptual content of perceptual experience: Situation dependence and fineness of grain. *Philosophy and Phenomenological Research* 62 (3): 601–608. Reprinted in *Essays on Nonconceptual Content*, ed. Y. Gunther. MIT Press.

Levine, J. 1983. Materialism and qualia: The explanatory gap. *Pacific Philosophical Quarterly* 64: 354–361.

Makin, G. 2000. *The Metaphysicians of Meaning*. Routledge.

McDowell, J. 1994. *Mind and World*. Harvard University Press.

McDowell, J. 2007a. Response to Dreyfus. *Inquiry* 50 (4): 366–370.

McDowell, J. 2007b. What myth? *Inquiry* 50 (4): 338–351.

McDowell, J. 2009. *Having the World in View: Essays on Kant, Hegel, and Sellars*. Harvard University Press.

McGinn, C. 1989. *Mental Content*. Blackwell.

Marr, D. 1982. *Vision: A Computational Investigation into the Human Representation and Processing of Visual Information*. Freeman.

Menary, R. 2007. *Cognitive Integration: Mind and Cognition Unbounded*. Palgrave.

Menary, R. 2010a. Cognitive integration and the extended mind. In *The Extended Mind*, ed. R. Menary. MIT Press.

Menary, R. 2010b. Introduction: The extended mind in focus. In *The Extended Mind*, ed. R. Menary. MIT Press.

Millikan, R. G. 1984. *Language, Thought, and Other Biological Categories*. MIT Press.

Millikan, R. G. 1993. *White Queen Psychology and Other Essays for Alice*. MIT Press.

Millikan, R. G. 2004. *Varieties of Meaning: The 2002 Jean Nicod Lectures*. MIT Press.

Millikan, R. G. 2005. *Language: A Biological Model*. Oxford University Press.

Millikan, R. G. 2006. Useless content. In *Teleosemantics*, ed. G. Macdonald and D. Papineau. Oxford University Press.

Milner, D., and Goodale, M. 1995. *The Visual Brain in Action*. Oxford University Press.

Myin, E., and O'Regan, J. K. 2009. Situated perception and sensation in vision and other modalities: A sensorimotor approach. In *The Cambridge Handbook of Situated Cognition*, ed. P. Robbins and M. Aydede. Cambridge University Press.

Neander, K. 2006. Content for cognitive science. In *Teleosemantics*, ed. G. Macdonald and D. Papineau. Oxford University Press.

Noë, A. 2004. *Action in Perception*. MIT Press.

Noë, A. 2009. *Out of Our Heads*. Hill and Wang.

Noë, A. 2012. *Varieties of Presence*. Harvard University Press.

O'Regan, J. K. 2011. *Why Red Doesn't Sound Like a Bell: Understanding the Feel of Consciousness*. Oxford University Press.

O'Regan, J. K., and Block, N. 2012. Discussion of J. Kevin O'Regan's *Why Red Doesn't Sound Like a Bell*. *Review of Philosophy and Psychology* 3 (1): 89–108.

O'Regan, J. K., and Noë, A. 2001. A sensorimotor account of vision and visual consciousness. *Behavioral and Brain Sciences* 24: 939–1031.

Papineau, D. 1987. *Reality and Representation*. Oxford University Press.

Papineau, D. 1993. *Philosophical Naturalism*. Blackwell.

Papineau, D. 2002. *Thinking about Consciousness*. Oxford University Press.

Prinz, J. 2006. Putting the brakes on enactive perception. *Psyche* 12 (1): 1–19.

Prinz, J. 2007. Mental pointing: Phenomenal knowledge without concepts. *Journal of Consciousness Studies* 14 (9–10): 184–211.

Prinz, J. 2009. Is consciousness embodied? In *The Cambridge Handbook of Situated Cognition*, ed. P. Robbins and M. Aydede. Cambridge University Press.

Ramsey, W. M. 2007. *Representation Reconsidered*. Cambridge University Press.

Roberts, T. 2010. Understanding 'sensorimotor understanding'. *Phenomenology and the Cognitive Sciences* 9 (1): 101–111.

Robbins, P., and Aydede, M. 2009. *The Cambridge Handbook of Situated Cognition*. Cambridge University Press.

Rowlands, M. 2003. *Externalism: Putting the Mind and World Back Together*. Acumen.

Rowlands, M. 2006. *Body Language*. MIT Press.

Ryder, D. 2006. On thinking of kinds: A neuroscientific perspective. In *Teleosemantics*, ed. G. Macdonald and D. Papineau. Oxford University Press.

Ryle, G. 1949. *The Concept of Mind*. Hutchinson.

Seager, W. 2000. *Theories of Consciousness*. Routledge.

Searle, J. 1984. *Minds, Brains, and Science*. Harvard University Press.

Searle, J. 1990. Is the brain a digital computer? *Proceedings and Addresses of the American Philosophical Association* 64 (November): 21–37.

Searle, J. 1992. *The Rediscovery of the Mind*. MIT Press.

Shannon, C. E. 1948. A mathematical theory of communication. *Bell System Technical Journal* 27: 379–423, 623–656.

Shapiro, L. 2011. *Embodied Cognition*. Routledge.

Speaks, J. 2005. Is there a problem about nonconceptual content? *Philosophical Review* 114: 359–398.

Stalnaker, R. 1998. What might nonconceptual content be? *Philosophical Issues* 9: 339–352.

Stanley, J., and Williamson, T. 2001. Knowing how. *Journal of Philosophy* 98 (8): 411–444.

Steiner, P. 2010. The bounds of representation. *Pragmatics and Cognition* 18 (2): 235–272.

Sterelny, K. 2010. Minds: Extended or scaffolded? *Phenomenology and the Cognitive Sciences* 9: 465–481.

Stich, S. 1990. *The Fragmentation of Reason: Preface to a Pragmatic Theory of Cognitive Evaluation*. MIT Press.

Strawson, G. 1994. *Mental Reality*. MIT Press.

Summers, J. J., and Anson, G. A. 2009. Current status of the motor programme revisited. *Human Movement Science* 28: 566–577.

Sutton, J. 2010. Exograms and interdisciplinarity: History, the extended mind, and the civilization process. In *The Extended Mind*, ed. R. Menary. MIT Press.

Tallis, R. 2003. *The Hand: A Philosophical Inquiry into Human Being*. Edinburgh University Press.

Thompson, E. 2007. *Mind in Life: Biology, Phenomenology, and the Sciences of Mind*. Harvard University Press.

Tye, M. 1996. *Ten Problems of Consciousness: A Representational Theory of the Phenomenal Mind*. MIT Press.

Tye, M. 2009. *Consciousness Revised: Materialism without Phenomenal Concepts*. MIT Press.

Van Gelder, T. 1995. What might cognition be if not computation? *Journal of Philosophy* 91: 345–381.

Varela, F., Thompson, E., and Rosch, F. 1991. *The Embodied Mind: Cognitive Science and Human Experience*. MIT Press.

Velleman, J. D. 2000. *The Possibility of Practical Reason*. Oxford University Press.

Ward, D. Enjoying the spread: Consciousness externalism revisited. *Mind*, in press.

Webb, B. 1994. Robotic experiments in cricket phototaxis. In *From Animals to Animats 3: Proceedings of the Third Annual Conference on Simulation of Adaptive Behaviour*, ed. D. Cliff et al. MIT Press.

Webb, B. 1996. A cricket robot. *Scientific American* 275 (6): 62–67.

Weiskopf, D. 2008. Patrolling the mind's boundaries. *Erkenntnis* 68: 265–276.

Wheeler, M. 2005. *Reconstructing the Cognitive World*. MIT Press.

Wheeler, M. 2008. Minimal representing: A response to Gallagher. *International Journal of Philosophical Studies* 16 (3): 371–376.

Williams, M. 2010. *Blind Obedience. The Structure and Content of Wittgenstein's Later Philosophy*. Routledge.

Wilson, R. A. 1994. Wide computationalism. *Mind* 103: 351–372.

Wilson, R. A. 2010. Meaning making and the mind of the externalist. In *The Extended Mind*, ed. R. Menary. MIT Press.

Index